Journey to Joy

A Course about
Living and Being in Joy

Jannie Bennett

iUniverse, Inc.
Bloomington

Journey to Joy
A Course about Living and Being in Joy

Note: *This course reflects only the personal experiences and views of the author. The information contained herein is for educational purposes only.*

iUniverse books may be ordered through booksellers or by contacting:

iUniverse
1663 Liberty Drive
Bloomington, IN 47403
www.iuniverse.com
1-800-Authors (1-800-288-4677)

ISBN: 978-1-4620-0323-5 (sc)
ISBN: 978-1-4620-0324-2 (e)
ISBN: 978-1-4620-0322-8 (hc)

Library of Congress Control Number: 2011904122

Printed in the United States of America

iUniverse rev. date: 12/1/2011

To my wonderful family,
thank you for the divine gift you are to my life.
I love you forever and always.

*J*ourney to *J*oy
Course Contents

Part II *How to Initiate Change*

Part III *Using the Course Material*

Part IV *Journey to Joy Stories*

You cannot LOVE what you haven't experienced.
Come experience what you are going to LOVE.

Journey to Joy
with

Tannie Bennett

Preface

The miracle of life is what is recorded in the heart.
When you change the heart, you change the man.

My Personal Experience with This Work
This journey to joy we are about to embark on, I can honestly say, I have been on all of my life. I set this intention even before I came to earth to live. My intention then was to return to my Father in Heaven, which is a place of pure joy. So I have been at this job for a very long time.

Even though I have been heading in the direction of joy, I have not been conscious of this journey quite as long as I have been on it. Basically, I was fumbling around in the dark for some time, which—believe it or not—is actually a part of the journey to joy.

We start our lives on earth experiencing opposition and contrast. Then, after we have had enough opposition, we turn to our Father in Heaven and pray for help. I became conscious of my journey to joy when I reached the point of desperately wanting change. I knew I wanted to be in joy and to have different life experiences. By this time, I was ready and ripe for change; I had finally reached the point where remaining the same was no longer an option. There was no turning back; it was change or bust. I turned to Heavenly Father and prayed my heart out to Him. The heavens opened, and I received the assistance I needed to become more of what I dreamed of in my earliest beginnings—a joy-filled, happy, loving person.

The course seemed long at times. I wanted a miracle—the kind of miracle that occurred in biblical times. I knew that if I had faith, it was possible. It was in these early beginnings that I learned I was to take the long road. I was not only going for my benefit but in time I was to assist others on the same journey. In order to do so, I needed to know the path well. So I rolled up my sleeves and began my journey, letting go of time expectations and trusting God's will.

The most significant thing I noticed in these early periods was that my life was no longer the same. I began to experience real change. I struggled at times, but these times did not last long and neither did the pain of the experience. In fact, the longer I was on the path to joy, the better it got. Soon, I loved waking up in the morning; I could hardly wait to get on with the day. I became focused; joy was the goal, and I knew I was moving in that direction. It felt so good. Next, my focus turned to my family. I wanted my entire family to be on the same path because it was so fun. It didn't take long to learn that the way to get my family involved was to simply stay on the road myself. When they saw my joy, they would want to come along.

We did have moments of adjustment, though, the most significant of which were probably for my older children, who were living away from home. Each time they came home, they returned to a totally different energy and a totally different mom. This was unsettling to them, but soon they realized that even though home was different, it was good. Then they too began to flow with the changes.

As I continued on my path, I noticed that my family was speaking my language and singing my songs. It was delightful. One of my earliest memories of family change occurred one evening as I was driving up our street headed for home. I noticed a group of neighborhood children gathered. I sensed that there was a difficult situation and pulled up beside the group. I then heard my son, who was probably eleven at the time, counseling these young children in wisdom and love, saying things I had said to him. This brought me great joy. He was getting it!

I also remember wondering if I was ever going to complete my journey. I just wanted to get there; I just wanted to be happy. I soon learned that the goal was traveling through life feeling joy. This was the feeling that was to accompany me each day of my life's journey. This I could achieve in the very moment I thought it. What a great moment of insight that was.

After that moment, my journey changed from longing for the destination to trying to stay on the road. Then it progressed to maintaining that joy-filled state throughout the day. As I journeyed along my path to joy, I recorded my experiences in my journal. This practice also became a significant part of my learning process.

Later, the Spirit made it known to me that I was to write a book. This took a great deal of time. I wrote things that I didn't know or have a working knowledge of at the time. This was my course material, my lessons from the Spirit. I completed the rough draft in about six months and then began to edit my writings. It was during the editing process, as I read and reread my book, that it all began to sink in.

As I was working on the written form of the course material, I was very actively engaged in rapid-eye technology, a process that releases negative programming. This too was part of my schooling and preparation. I not only learned how to help others release stress and change their core beliefs, but I was very active in my own release work, doing personal sessions for myself or my family weekly. This process I loved as well. From the beginning, I had wonderful experiences as a result of this work—experiences so sacred that I have shared them with only a few. The journey was indeed becoming more joyful.

Time passed and my joy increased. I became conscious of something new to my life's experience. I began waking up feeling so great that I just wanted to call someone on the phone to tell him or her how happy I was. I felt at times I was going to burst with joy. In the beginning, it was infrequent, but these experiences alone kept me moving forward. I began to wonder, *Can life really be this good? Can my life hold this much happiness?* If you were to look around my environment, you would not have seen much of a physical difference. I lived in the same house, on the same street, and did pretty much the same things. I had the same responsibilities; I was still a mother raising my family, but I was not the same person inside. I was refreshed and new. I had found the "refresh" button to my life's computer, which was being pressed daily, and I loved it.

Now the Spirit has directed me to move on and to get this information out so that you too might experience this kind of "kick your feet up, feel like you're going to burst inside" joy, that you too might journey through your life in joy.

God has blessed us so abundantly. Becoming conscious of this was part of my joy-filled journey. I began to see the world with different eyes; I began to see the world as a wonderful place to live. Yes, there were difficult things going on around me, but not in me. Inside, my world was at peace. I began to live in "the millennium," which is a time of peace.

I remember the times of war. I remember the battle cries inside of myself. I remember the hate, the abuse, the fear, and the sadness. I remember the pain and the loneliness and the feeling of wanting to run away to end it all. I remember hurting so badly inside that I felt my heart was going to crack. I remember crying for days without rest. I remember it all. But now my joy is complete because it is all just a memory and not my life. It was my experience, but it is not who I am. I am so much more than these experiences, but it was from these experiences that I became aware of who I really am and that I am so much more.

My intention in sharing my personal journey with you, and sharing a part of my past, is to help you know that I am sincere. It is my heartfelt desire to assist you on your journey to joy.

I am at peace; my world is at peace. Though I do not see your face now, I feel we were meant to be together. I have made many contracts with many of my brothers and sisters in Heavenly Father's family, and if you are reading or experiencing this work, then it is quite possible that you are one of them. I have come into contact with many that I knew in my pre-earth life because of this path I am on, and it has brought great joy to my heart as we have become reunited. In each instance, this remembrance has come to us both.

As you participate in this course, you will discover your remembrance. Once you become clear of your personal battlefields and it is quiet within, you will discover many great treasures—treasures that have been there all along but because you were actively engaged in these wars within, you were unable to see or discover them.

The journey to joy is a journey of peace, which will come as you win your wars, quiet your cries, meet your needs, and feel love once again. These positive feelings may seem foreign to you now, but they are as much a part of you as the negative feelings you feel inside; it is just that you are unaware of them because of your battles.

It is time to experience the joys of life. It is time to experience the opposite of what you have been experiencing and to learn how to live your life "in joy."

Join me in this magnificent process, one that can change your present reality into a wonderful life filled with peace and joy.

Tannie Bennett

Acknowledgments

This course was a gift to my life, a gift from above. Therefore, I would like to acknowledge my heavenly crew for its assistance. I received a great deal of help in the construction of the course. Although I have felt my weaknesses in receiving this information, I know of its source because I have always trusted in this part of my life. I have always trusted God and knew He had a significant role in guiding me throughout my life. This course information is a result of the guidance I have received.

I would like to extend love and appreciation to my family for their love and support. I have spent untold hours at the computer and in sessions and classes as I personally experienced the information I am presenting to you. My family is truly one of my greatest joys and my greatest gift.

Special thanks go to Ranae Johnson, founder of the Rapid Eye Institute; my Rapid Eye family; and my clients for their role in my education and training. I would also like to thank T. J. Eich and Barbie Hansen, my cover models; my editors, Patrick Bennett, Christie Jones, Norm Jackson, and Jennifer Jackson; my proofreaders, Judy Staley, and Debra Bennett; and my early course members for their work and service. I would like to thank Amy Beck, Danni Jackson, and Amber Lee Newsom for their photographic talents and contributions to the book. I would also like to acknowledge and thank Dale Devers at Inside Out Productions, who worked over the holiday to make this happen, as well as Perry Bingham of Sunnybrook Video, creator and composer of the music in the first imagery CD, and Jamie Glaser for his musical composition on the second imagery CD. I would also like to thank Shauna Sprunger for her many talents in layout and recording. My dear friend Raland Brunson at Rose Pedal Records I can hardly thank enough for his many hours of personal tutoring, music, support, and hard work. I so appreciate my dearest friends Sylvia Franklin, Leah Staley and Marcelle Stegelmeier, who faithfully supported me on my personal journey to joy. Their positive, clear voices kept me up and moving forward. I truly don't know what I would have done without them. I would also like to thank Danni Jackson, Carol Goodwin, and Glenda Henthorn for their contributions, love, and support and for taking this journey with me. Thank you. I appreciate and love you all.

Introduction

Where Our Journey Began

A long time ago, before you were born, you lived in another place and another time. You lived with your Heavenly Father and Heavenly Mother. You were their spirit offspring.

You were very much alive in your heavenly home. You achieved many glorious and wonderful accomplishments. Your family loved and honored your greatness.

Then came the dawn of a new time in the eternities. It was a time of great excitement and great anticipation, for all of the heavens rejoiced at the plan that was presented. The plan was one of progress and empowerment. This plan would enable you to become like your Father and Mother in Heaven. This plan afforded you the opportunity to gain a physical body that was unlike your spirit body but fashioned after its likeness.

The purpose in obtaining this body was to become more like your eternal parents, who possessed both physical and spiritual bodies, though their bodies were perfected and redeemed.

The day this plan was presented, the heavens wept for joy, and a great heavenly choir sang songs of rejoicing. The trust of our Heavenly King was great. To think that He loved us so much that He desired us to have the opportunity to achieve His great and glorious state caused unimaginable rejoicing.

The plan was to create an earth of physical elements, the same elements that composed Father and Mother's glorious bodies. The creator of the earth was Father's first-born son, Jesus Christ. He, along with the help of the Archangel Michael and under the direction of the Father, was sent to accomplish this great and marvelous work. All of the spirits watched this amazing creation unfold.

At the completion of the earth, Father announced that the work was good. He blessed the earth and then announced His plan to people it. He informed us that we would be sent down a few at a time in the beginning, and then as time progressed more would be allowed to follow.

Earth began her journey. The earth was composed of love elements, which contained intelligence. This was as it had always been through the eons of time. The elements of the earth were to be the same elements that would make up our physical bodies. Heavenly Father pronounced it good.

Adam was the first, and then Eve. Then the process of procreation began. Adam and Eve began to people the earth. Eve became known as the Mother of All Living, and we honored her greatness. When Eve began to have her children, because her food consisted of the elements of the earth, her children's bodies would contain these very elements. So the creation of mankind began.

The earth progressed, and more and more children were born upon the earth. At the birth of each child, Heavenly Father and Mother would send a spirit down to possess the body that was formed. The body became the physical temple or tabernacle of the spirit. The spirit child of Heavenly Father and Heavenly Mother would reside in the bodies Adam and Eve created through the process of human birth.

Time passed.

Many, many spirit children have come to live and die upon the earth. As their bodies grew old and their earthly schooling was completed, Father and Mother would call them home. Their bodies would return to the elements from which they came, and their spirits would return to heaven. This was all part of the plan.

Father planned many more great and glorious things for us to experience on the earth, but the most significant one was to experience the physical body. Having a physical body would be very different from having the spiritual one we experienced as a spirit in the heavens. Having a physical body would be a type of schooling, a testing time. It would be a time that we could learn from our own choices the cause-and-effect principle. It would be a time we could experience many, many principles that Father taught. We could have no concept of these principles until we were in a physical body. We could not know true joy without experiencing its opposite. Therefore, He set up a "school of opposition." This would be a testing time to see if we would again choose to live the truths we were taught in the heavens. On earth we would have opposition to contend with. We all had a choice; Father left it all up to us to decide whether we desired to participate in this experience.

Many spirit children chose to come, and some chose to stay. Those who chose to come to earth were given many great and glorious gifts from Father to help them on their journeys. Each spirit that came to earth would always have agency (the ability to choose for oneself), as it was in the heavens. Agency is an eternal law that cannot be broken.

As the spirits came to the earth to experience agency, they would experience the life they chose while in the heavens. Each spirit was given the opportunity to choose what it wanted to experience while upon the earth. Father taught the spirits, as they made their choices, everything they needed to know before they left the heavens. He encoded these choices in their records and within the DNA in their bodies. These choices and contracts were agreed upon, and then we, the spirits, made a covenant with Father to fulfill them. We were not left alone in this. Father provided systems within our bodies to help us move forward with these contracts.

If we chose to experience pain, that was set. If we chose to experience love, that too was set. All emotions, both positive and negative, were set in our contracts as we chose these experiences. Father also taught us the effect of these choices. If we wanted certain blessings in heaven, certain experiences would be required. We each chose our blessings and our experiences. Father, in His wisdom, assisted with much of the process.

As we came to earth, our experiences began. To complete our contracts would require certain knowledge, but each of us would be gifted with much heavenly help, if we needed it. All we would have to do is ask.

You are now upon the earth experiencing the contracts you have made. Many are feeling the weight and pain of these contracts. I have come to teach you how to move forward in your contracts and to help you learn how to complete them in joy.

We have experienced much opposition in the history of the earth, and now is the dawning of a new age. Now is the time of fulfillment of these contracts.

I will teach you throughout this course the process of healing, how to find out what your contracts are, and how to heal your life from the pain of your opposition—the pain that you and your ancestors have come through.

For now begins the cleansing and the healing of the earth and the inhabitants that have been placed on it. This time has been spoken of from the beginning. This time is the time of "the great and dreadful day of the Lord" (Mal. 4:5 King James Version) It is a time of cleansing and healing the earth and the inhabitants thereon.

My intention is to help the day be a great one for you, not a dreadful one. My intention is to help you heal your life and cleanse it so you may go forth and rejoice in the day of His coming. Be patient with the process for it will take time. But as you heed these instructions, you will heal your life.

I have been sent to show you the way to heal your life by healing my own. I have been sent to help Father in His great and glorious work. As you participate in the imageries with full purpose of heart and do the exercises with all diligence, you will heal.

Note: *A recording of the imageries and affirmations in this course can be found in the complete audio version of this book. They are also available as a two disc set at Tannie Bennett's web site.*

An extended version of the practice exercises can be found in the student workbook.

Part I

Beginning the Journey

Healing is...

Remembering
Who you are and
returning to the vibration
from which you have come
Tonnie Bennett

1
Understanding Why We Are Here

We have been alive for a long time, but most of us aren't really living. We are just barely getting by, and we are not very happy. Think about your own life for a minute. Are you happy?

You may be happy at times, but when you aren't, what is it that makes you feel dissatisfied with life? What makes you feel like you don't want to go home, you don't want to go to work, or you don't want to face another day? Maybe you don't even want to wake up; you just want to sleep all day. Have you thought about what causes you to feel that way?

What is the root cause of your misery, unhappiness, or depression?

We all have a desire to be happy. Most of us have experienced moments of joy and happiness. But are we happy most of the time, or are there days when we don't even crack a smile?

While journeying through life, we have experienced happiness and unhappiness. We have had moments of pleasure and pain. We have experienced every emotion known. But did you know that experiencing all these emotions was one of the very purposes for which you came into this realm of existence? You came here ("here" meaning earth) to feel—more specifically to feel the feelings of the physical body. Feeling in a physical body was something you had never experienced as a spirit in the heavens, and you desired to have that experience. In fact, you wanted it so badly that you could hardly wait for your turn.

Before you came to earth for your experience here, you were pure light and perfect intelligence. You were more in your pre-earth life than your finite mind at this point can even imagine. You were the perfect offspring of God. You were the spirit child of the Great Eternal Being, the Great Eloheim, the Great I AM. Can you even imagine the greatness of God? If you can, then you can imagine the greatness of you. You were literally the spirit offspring of God.

Now, for some that may be a big bite to chew, but consider it. It really is wonderful to imagine being a great and powerful, perfect being. Can you wrap your mind around it? Spend a moment thinking about that magnificent thought. Try it out.

For some, this is not a new thought but a familiar one. Even so, I would encourage you to stop for a moment and wrap your thoughts around the magnificence of being the offspring of God. It is a pretty significant thought, and it is a very important one for our subject today.

Assuming that you have stopped and taken time to get into the thought place of being the literal offspring of God, let's move forward a little further.

Considering the possibility of coming to earth to feel may be a new thought, but coming here to feel is a very significant experience and part of your purpose for being here.

Having the ability to feel is a very important part of being like your eternal spirit parents. It is truly a part of being a God. It is one of the most important elements of your earthly experience.

You may be wondering why I am going on about the importance of feeling. Well, if it is our desire to be happy and to have a happy, joy-filled life, then don't you think feeling is important? Of course it is. So what about all the "bad" stuff?

Is that important to feel as well, or can we just experience the good stuff?

Imagine for a moment that you are an artist, and the only color you have to work with is white. What kind of picture would you paint? I imagine it would not be a very interesting one, but if you were to add the color black, then you could do so much with the contrast. You could create some very interesting art. In fact, with just the two colors, you could create for a very long time. Now imagine for a moment that the varieties of feelings are represented by all of the other colors and that this array is added to your palette. You would then have an infinite opportunity to create, and this magnificent array could take you well into forever. Think of the incredible variety of creations you have seen in your lifetime. It is quite amazing when you consider what you have already seen.

Continue to focus on your palette filled with numerous colors. You are now settling in to create a magnificent work of art. Wouldn't you experience tremendous joy knowing you had so many possibilities before you? There would be no limit as to what you could create on your canvas because of the infinite choices of color, right? Well, that's what you saw when you chose to come to earth. You saw an infinite array of feelings, and you wanted to experience them. You wanted to experience it all. You knew that from contrast, great works are created.

The contrast of light and dark is what makes a picture beautiful. It is the contrast of light and dark that will make you into the masterpiece you intended to be in your beginnings.

Before you came to earth you were already pure light, pure love, and pure intelligence. How could you improve on such perfection? There was no need to improve on perfection, to improve on who you were at that point. The only choice was to add to the perfection, to add another dimension to you. So God, in all his wisdom, gave us the incredible opportunity to add the physical element to our perfection, to add the experience

5

of being in the physical body so that we could feel and enjoy everything that the experience had to offer.

When the plan of creating an earth and having the opportunity to inhabit this earth was presented, we all wept for joy because, in our premortal state, we understood the magnificence of this opportunity. We wanted this experience. We wanted the experience of being in a physical body, and we wanted the experience of creating in this realm. What a joy this was to us.

If you are still with me on this, then imagine the first time you experienced contrast, when all you were used to was pure light. Imagine the first time you saw your pure white canvas being spotted with a contrasting color. I imagine that it might have been a real shock to see and experience something other than pure light and love.

Well, indeed it was!

When you left the spirit realm, you were magnificent. You were pure greatness. You came here to feel and experience contrast, and for you that contrast began in the very beginning of your life. It began when your physical experience began. The contrast began because you entered a lower, denser realm. You were entering a world of clay. Your physical body was composed of the elements of the earth, and it was very different from the experience you had while you were a spirit in the heavens. But remember, it was the experience you desired. You wanted to have the ability to create, and in order to have that ability you needed the whole array of choices. You needed all of the colors to choose from. You wanted to progress and to add to your perfection. Your intention was to be like your heavenly parents, who possessed both perfect spirit bodies and perfect physical bodies. To be like those whom you esteemed so greatly caused immense joy.

Leaving the spirit realm to come to earth was like leaving for school the first time. You were excited about the opportunity and the growth but a bit apprehensive about this totally new experience. When you came to earth, the contrast began. You began to "feel."

This experience was an experience in feeling. You would now feel what it was like to be in a physical body, to be in a tabernacle of clay. You would feel what it was like to have your array of contrasting experiences. Remember, this was what you wanted. If you didn't, you would not be here because agency is an eternal law that God Himself honors. You must have choice in this matter. We did have choice, and from our spirit perspective we thought it was a great plan. Now we are here experiencing our physical perspective, and we often question our choice.

We began to question the experience because of the contrast we felt. We had great contrast; we had love and hate, pain and pleasure, hope and despair—we had the entire palette of feelings. Now we are in the middle of the experience, and most of us wake up not wanting the experience anymore. We are tired of the contrast; we are tired of all the battles we fight, all the pain we feel, all the guilt, frustration, anger, hate, illness, abuse, neglect, and loneliness. We are screaming, "Stop, world! I want to get off! I don't want this experience anymore. I want to go home. I am tired of all the battles. Just let me die."

Have you ever felt anything like that before? Most likely you have. Why else would you be reading a book about how to be happy or how to be in joy?

Here is the good news: you can stop the contrast. You can stop the pain and the battles, and here's how.

The reason the contrast feels the way it does now is that you have not let go of your early perceptions and beliefs about the contrast. We came here to feel and experience contrast, but we do not have to stay in those feelings. We can move past them and on to more pleasant ones. We can have a totally new experience by simply letting go of those first perceptions about our experience. For example, have you ever jumped into a swimming pool and felt the shock of the temperature variance

7

between your warm body and the cold water? After a moment of being in the water, you adjust and then you can enjoy your swimming experience.

But how do you know you can adjust? You know you can adjust because you have had the experience of adjusting. Within a few short minutes of being in the water, you know that you will come into balance with the temperature and won't feel the cold. Well, imagine how your swimming experience would be if you stayed in that shock mode or that first-moment experience. My guess is that you would not enjoy your swimming experience and perhaps never go in the water again. But the good news is that we do adjust and things do get better. Now imagine for a moment that, for some reason, your life-recording button got stuck on that shock moment. Do you think it would influence your relationship with water and swimming? I am quite sure it would.

Our contrast, or our earthly experience, is tainted to a great extent by our first shock moments. We have had many such moments in life, and they have colored our world with a murky medley of negativity. As an adult, you know that you will eventually adjust to the water temperature and you can stick it out until that happens because your intention is to have a great time swimming. So it is with life. As an adult, you know a lot about life that you didn't know as a child, an infant, or a new spirit being experiencing the physical body for the first time. You didn't know the very first time you experienced cold that it would soon warm up. You didn't know in your first experience with pain that you would heal. You didn't know during your first experience with being alone that your parents would return. All you were left with was the experience of that "shocked feeling."

Your life progressed, and through experience you soon learned that pain heals, Mom and Dad come back, winter turns into spring, and life gets better.

How did you learn that? Through your experience.

What about the "shock experiences"? They are still in us waiting to be completed.

What do I mean by "completed?"

It's quite like that first dot of black paint on your white canvas; it can be pretty ugly unless something is done with it. When you begin to move the paint around and add to the experience more skill, knowledge, and time, it can become a beautiful work of art. Yet if it is just left as a blob, it will affect the beauty and wonder of your life's creation. You came here to create and to feel the wonder of the experience, not just experience the shock of the contrast.

What we are experiencing now, our great opposition experiences, is the painful result of those shock moments. Each experience is not truly complete until you can stand back, look at what you have created, and feel awe, thinking, *That is magnificent!*

Can you now look at any part of your life and feel the magic of your creations? Can you look in awe at what you have learned and what you have become? If you cannot, then the only message I have for you today is that your work is not complete. If you are still living in pain, anger, and loneliness on any level, your work is not complete. This is the message of this course. I am here to teach you how to bring your masterpiece into view. I am here to teach you how to complete what you have come here to do and how to feel the magic and wonder of your magnificent life. I am here to help you capture the vision of your greatness, the vision of your work completed.

Your work will be complete when you can see yourself as your Father in Heaven sees you, when you can love yourself as your eternal family loves you and once again feel the majesty of being the divine child of God that you are.

Join me on this marvelous journey of completing the purpose of your life, of coming into your magnificence and divinity, and of experiencing and celebrating that on a daily basis.

Life is wonderful! It is filled with purpose and meaning but only for those who seek to see and experience the masterpiece that lies within.

2

How We Are Programmed for Our Life Experiences

Can We Change the Programming?

The day you were born was a very special day. It was an important day for everyone.

Your mother of course was there, along with other significant people anxiously awaiting your arrival. As the anticipation of your birth moment arrived, there was much excitement in the air. For some, it was just another birth, but for you, it was the most significant moment of your life up to that point.

When the birthing process began, the little bundle of perfection inside the mother's womb was awaiting the event. This indeed was something you had never experienced before and something you would never experience again. We are only given one birth experience, so the importance of this moment is significant.

You probably have never considered looking at birth in this way. We usually look at the birthing process from the mother's, father's, or doctor's point of view, but few have given thought as to what it is like for the infant.

The purpose and intent of this writing is to focus on the significance of the birthing process for the infant from its own perspective. Typically, we believe that because of an infant's limited capacity to communicate and its underdeveloped brain, there is not much going on. But what I am about to share may change your perceptions. This information certainly changed the direction of my life.

From the moment of conception to the moment of birth and beyond, the infant is very much alive and active in its environment. The infant has the ability to perceive and feel absolutely everything that the mother, father, and family experience. The infant actually makes conclusions about life itself.

This is important because these conclusions formed in the infant's mind are the very programs that make up the life experiences of that individual. For instance, if the infant perceives at the time of conception that it is unwanted and a burden, then these beliefs actually create to a great extent the life experiences of that individual. If the infant perceives that it is welcomed and a wonderful surprise, then these perceptions affect the individual as well.

All conclusions that the infant forms become the infant's core programming and life script.

These early beliefs are cemented in the infant's life script and create future experiences based upon these perceptions. These are the programs that the infant's brain runs on or is programmed with for the rest of its life or until the individual becomes aware of the programming and decides it is time for a new program.

You can have a new program anytime you are ready. Usually it is not until we are doing a face plant in the pavement of life that we are awakened to the fact that life is not fun. We realize then that we really need to make some major changes because we are not going to survive many more of these painful experiences.

When we awaken to the fact that we can change our lives and that there is an easy way to reprogram our original programming, it is definitely a high-five moment. It usually takes some very painful experiences on our part, and we may have to experience them not only once or twice but multiple times before we awaken to the fact that we have done this enough and wonder how we are going to change. I personally tried to change direction many, many times without success before I became doggedly determined that I was going to find a way or bust.

I found the way! And that is what I intend to share with you in this course.

This course is all about changing our life's programming. There is much to our programming or life's script that gets in the way of our happiness and success. It is made up of not only what we perceived but also what our parents and others close around us perceived and felt during our birth and early childhood experience.

In the process of assisting my clients change their core programming, I have run into many very interesting programs, each one unique and significant to the individual. Once these programs are set in as core beliefs, they are then played out throughout the individual's life and supported by the ego to keep them active and in place. You see, the brain doesn't care what is put into it. It is like our computer. It makes no judgment of whether or not something will work. The mind will simply play out the program and keep doing so until you, the programmer, decide it is time for a change.

The only—I repeat—the *only* way to make a permanent life change is to change your core programming. Change your subconscious beliefs about life. Change those shock moments.

If you have ever tried to change just by thinking you wanted to and you have come up with a really great plan and worked up a ton of willpower, most likely you discovered that willpower is not enough. Willpower is not what it takes to change your core programming.

Perhaps at that time you heard your friends or family comment, "All you need is to try a little harder, and you can do it!" So then you surmise, "Well, I guess something is wrong with me because I thought I was trying. I have tried many different things over the years and still I have not found success. Something must be really wrong. I must really be weak and lacking because I just can't do this." Then because of the number of failed attempts, you add a new negative load to your already-full core programming bank account.

When is enough enough? Aren't you tired of trying to change your life without getting the success you feel you deserve? If all it took was trying a little harder, believe me, you would have changed your life successfully years and years ago. Willpower is not the key. Changing your core programming is.

Most of our core programming was set during the very beginning of our life experiences. These are the patterns that keep knocking you on your fanny; these are the thorns in your side, your roadblocks. This is what you want to look at and change in order to get the lasting transformation you really desire.

How do you rewrite your core programming or life script? How can you once and for all get rid of those stumbling blocks that are keeping you from the relationships, success, love, and happiness that you deserve?

That is what this course is all about—teaching you how to change these programs and how to get into the part of your brain that holds them. Then, after you reprogram your brain, the course will teach you how to successfully move forward to begin to live the life you have always wanted but have been unable to achieve up until now.

Change can be an elegant and gentle process. You no longer need to beat yourself up for not having the strength to make the changes that you have longed to make. It does not require strength, nor does it require willpower. All it requires is a little bit of knowledge, a few new yet ever-so-simple skills, and a continued desire to keep at it until you have arrived at the place in life you have longed to be.

The greatest part about this course is that when you begin using these simple techniques, you will feel they are familiar and that you have done them before.

Once you begin the process of change and begin to see how significantly you can affect your own transformation in life and actually see, feel, and experience these changes, then you will be in a great position to spread the good news that change is easy and life can actually be fun.

A word of caution, though—change does take time, so please be kind to yourself. This is not the time to beat yourself up for not doing it. That's the old you, and there is no place in this program for self-abuse. This program is about loving yourself and taking care of one of God's greatest miracles— you.

Warning!

When you begin this program of change, there will be times that you will feel discouraged and like you are not doing it right or are not making the changes that you want to make. You will question yourself and your ability to change. I am sharing this with you now to warn you that these are the very programs or beliefs we are trying to change. Once you start to go into this type of thinking, be forewarned that this is what we will be looking for. This type of stinky thinking is what we want to bring to resolution. We want to change any thought or prerecorded message that creates within you feelings that are in opposition to joy.

Joy is our goal. When you play out programs that keep you from this goal, it will feel really bad. When you feel this way, then it is time to stop and question what is going on. In the past, we would just plunge into the negative life experiences and feelings, but no longer! Now we are going to stop at each one and bring these thoughts to resolution so we can get to where we want to be.

As mentioned before, this will take time, but that is okay. You won't mind because *you will feel the change.* You will know that what you are now doing is really making a difference. You will have the strength to move forward because you will be reinforced by the changes you experience. You'll say, "Finally! This time I'm making it. I am really, really changing."

Take it from me: experiencing lasting change gets really exciting. So are you ready to make some very significant changes in your life? Are you ready to learn how to reprogram your brain computer and get to where you want to go? Are you ready to stop seeking answers and get them yourself? If you are, then you are in the right place. Now you are really on your journey to joy!

Note: My course members have suggested that I remind you to read this warning often because it is easy to forget that negative emotion is an invitation to choose again.

3

Changing Your Life by Changing Your Thoughts

"For as he thinketh in his heart, so is he."
—Prov. 23:7 (KJV)

We are here on earth experiencing a type of schooling. We are here to experience opposition—the opposite of our heavenly home. We are here to gain a body, learn, grow, and progress. There are other reasons for being here, but today I would like to focus on one that might be new to you.

We are here on earth to learn to become like our Father in Heaven. That may not be such a new thought, but consider this: we are here to become a creator like our Father in Heaven. Jesus Christ, under the direction of the Father, created this earth and everything on it. If we are truly children of God, then we too are creators. This is part of our natural inheritance and birthright.

We are creators, and this earthly life is our schooling in creation. We first become the creator of our world or, in other words, our lives.

We are the creator of our lives.

Try that on. How does that make you feel?

If someone would have suggested this to me several years ago, I would have instantly rejected the thought. I would have thought, *Why, if I were the creator of my life, would I create my life to be a living hell when all I have ever wanted was to live in peace? How did I do that, and why would I do that? I did not create this painful life. In fact, I have spent my entire life praying for peace and praying to be healed. Why would I do that to myself? No, that can't be true.*

Now I have a new and different perspective. We are the creators of our lives. When we become aware of this and clear out and let go of the patterns and behaviors we don't like—when we clear our subconscious programs that are on autopilot, programs that are causing us grief, programs that are blocking our truth—and become responsible for them, then we are in a position to create something really powerful.

One significant reason we are here is to experience opposition. Our opposition begins the moment we come into existence. In fact, it is the beginning of life that is so painful and difficult for us. Here we are—this beautiful package of perfection. We have been developing and progressing in the spirit realm for a very long time, waiting for our turn. Finally, it arrives, and then as we come to earth, we are squeezed into a physical body that doesn't do anything. Nothing works right; we have no control over anything. Can you imagine how difficult that might be? Talk about opposition. What a challenge!

I imagine coming to earth might be like visiting a foreign country for the first time. Have you ever had the experience of trying to communicate with someone who does not speak your language? It is a difficult experience when there are no common words between you except maybe "hello" and "yes." But there is body language. Universally, we all know how to smile, and with it something is communicated. We know how to cry, and this communicates. We all know emotional language.

This difficult situation is where we were when we were infants. Being in a body was a new experience. We needed to learn how to operate it from scratch. We needed to learn how to get our needs known and met, and we needed to learn how to communicate all our desires. We also needed to learn how to use our voices. Through our first painful breath, we instinctively learned how to cry and that we could make noise, and so with this simple skill, we began our experience. For a very long time, this was our only skill. We had little control over our bodies. Our arms would wave about; sometimes we would even hit ourselves in the face. Are you getting the picture of what a baby goes through? The beginning of life is pretty tough. Then to add to all of this original frustration, there are instances of abuse and neglect. Yes, being small is definitely experiencing opposition in its finest form.

Do you remember when you were small? All you wanted was to grow up. You always wanted to be bigger. You even pretended to be older, hoping to somehow, at least for a short playtime, be in charge.

We would even go so far as stretching our age out to ten and a half, or ten and three quarters. Then when we got ever so close to eleven, we would just say we were eleven. It wasn't about being a kid; it was all about being big and grown up. Why? Because we believed that when we grew up, we could do what we wanted to do.

Well, the day finally arrives—first eighteen and then twenty-one—and we are off. But what happens? We grew up to get to do what we wanted to do, but something we didn't consider or even think about before occurred. We realize that even though we are all grown up, we are still not doing what we want to do. Why? We believe that it's because if we want to eat, we need that job. If we want to play, we need money and time. If we want this, we need that. Our lives become really complicated, but we adjust and keep moving forward.

The years pass, and as we stop to look back, we ask ourselves, "Why is life not working for me?"

When we finally stop, we begin to search for peace, joy, love, success, and everything we have always wanted and have not been able to lay our hands on. For most of our lives, we have wanted to choose for ourselves and to just be happy, but there has been something in the way of our happiness—always something.

What is in the way of our happiness?

When we were little, what blocked our happiness is that we were little and couldn't communicate our needs or have our own way. Now that we are big, strangely, the very thing that is in the way of our happiness is being little. Think about that.

What is in the way of happiness now?

What's in the way of our happiness now is all the fractured parts of us—all our memories, misconceptions, and family patterns. When you were small, you experienced opposition, possibly even trauma. It could have been real or perceived; all you knew was that "this is not comfortable." In fact, it may have been very painful. At this time, you wanted the discomfort and pain to stop. So what did you do? What happened then?

In that moment in time, you actually did stop. You wanted the experience to stop because of how it felt, and so in an effort to stop the feeling, you stopped breathing and then the situation or the memory was frozen in time. When you stopped breathing, you were trying in the only way you knew to stop life itself. You figured that if you stopped your breath, you could stop life, but it never worked. You kept living, and the pain didn't go away.

So what did you do with the pain? You felt it, and you wanted it to go away. It didn't, so what did you do with it?

You instinctively stored it. (Refer to Chapter 14 *And It Came to Pass* for more understanding of how we store energy.) The energy of these painful experiences, the memories, was literally frozen in time. If the experience was extremely painful, you used your defense mechanisms to protect yourself from the pain. You became very creative in where you stored this information and pain. Some individuals who have experienced severe trauma develop alternative personalities to protect their core selves. Some of us build up walls in order to protect ourselves from these feelings. We have many defense mechanisms within.

These defense mechanisms we so effectively use were intended to help us survive. Heavenly Father sent us to our school of opposition with these mechanisms available for our use. The problem became magnified when our opposition became more than mere opposition and turned into painful abuse. This was not part of "the Plan," but because we were agents unto ourselves, we had the power to choose our experience.

Our opposition began to increase as we grew farther and farther away from Heavenly Father's original plan. That is the way of life. The farther we are away from the source of the light, the greater the darkness, or the greater our opposition becomes.

Through the course of time we were led off the path and onto paths of darkness because we forgot about our internal guidance system, a magnificent system Heavenly Father placed within us. How could we forget something so significant as our internal guidance system? Well, if we were not taught by the previous generation about the ins and outs of this system, then we would be left on our own to figure it out. Amazingly, many have figured it out, have learned to trust their instincts or their inner knowing, and have done well in life. But many have forgotten how to use this amazing system.

We were, however, able to survive our opposition and trauma because of the special defense mechanisms Heavenly Father placed within us. These systems were meant to be used only in an emergency; they were not intended to be used daily. Because we have strayed from God's teachings and have forgotten love as our focus, we have experienced far more opposition than necessary to complete the lessons we chose to experience.

We chose to come to earth to experience opposition, not abuse. But God, knowing man and his tendency to stray, provided support systems (defense mechanisms) to help us survive. And survive we have, but survival was not the intent of our existence. We needed to experience opposition but not to this extreme. It is time to change and to get back on the path. We will always experience opposition as we travel through life, but we can experience it in joy. Opposition is not abuse, and it was never God's intention for it to ever be so.

What about the painful memories that are frozen in time, the memories that our defense mechanisms so skillfully protected us from and tucked away? They are still there, waiting to be completed, waiting to be resolved.

Anytime we think a thought or develop a belief that is not in line with our truth or divine purpose, the thought is frozen in time. Many of these thoughts and memories are still waiting for you to act upon them. It is as if you hold them in your script book, and it now becomes requisite that these thoughts be acted upon. If the action we take is not in line with truth, the action will cause more opposition. If the action *is* in line with truth, then the thought and the action will bring us a great amount of joy.

We think many, many thoughts, and it is impossible to act on each and every one of them. But the actions we do take are not done in a way one might think. As your thoughts enter your mind, they come in the form of vibration. What is actually frozen in time is the vibration of the thought. If the thoughts that enter your mind are of a high vibration, then they will cause you to feel great joy. If the thoughts are of a lower vibration, they will cause you to feel a lower feeling, like sadness or depression. In this way, our thoughts are acted upon. We do not actually act out every thought that comes into our minds, but we do feel these thoughts as they register in us as vibrations. If we have had low-frequency thoughts for a very long time, then these thoughts begin to act upon and affect our physical bodies.

All lower vibrational thoughts, memories or beliefs are in need of resolution.

What is resolution, and how does this work? Resolution is the act that completes the thought process.

When a thought comes in at a very low vibration, this thought is frozen in us, waiting for resolution. Resolution comes when we actually realize that the thought is not in our best interest, and then we use our agency to change the thought to a higher-frequency thought. Everyone needs to go through this thought resolution process for every frozen thought.

In the spiritual milieu, this resolution process is known as repentance. The repentance process is actually a process of changing the thought's vibration from a lower one to a higher one. This occurs when we realize that this experience or thought is not what we want and then use our agency to choose again, at which point we choose a higher-vibration thought that is more aligned with what we do want.

Once, while reading the footnotes in a resource edition of the King James Version of the Bible, I discovered something very interesting. The Greek interpretation of the word *sin* is "misconception" or "misthought," and the Greek interpretation of the word *repentance* is "mind change." You are actually changing your mind or thoughts from a low vibration to a high vibration. Once we participate in the mind-changing process, our actions will then follow and we will be able to live and be in joy.

Our internal guidance system is the perfect indicator as to how we are doing. When we think thoughts that are not in line with our divine purpose, our guidance system sends out a warning and we feel the vibration of that thought. We literally feel low, down, or depressed. What we want is to become conscious of this process and tune into our warning system. When you start to feel low feelings or sense this warning signal, change your thoughts. Change them to higher-vibration thoughts. Change them to the highest vibration you can think of, and as you keep thinking high-vibration thoughts, you will start to feel up and joyful.

Now, what if you are receiving this information for the first time while feeling low all of the time and you haven't the faintest idea of where to begin? The first thing you do is start cleaning house. Start resolving some of your past, frozen thoughts. Your earliest thoughts are the ones with the weight because they have been in place the longest and have come in at a very strong vibration.

Your first experiences in opposition were your greatest. Remember, you had just left your heavenly home, had come to experience opposition, and those first experiences were real shockers. Think about the birthing process itself. Would you like to experience something like that again? We are blessed to only have to do that one once. Think about other times when you were little and you got into trouble when you really didn't mean to do anything wrong. You wouldn't want to repeat these experiences again either.

Have you ever wondered why you don't remember much of your childhood? It is because we block most of our memories because of how they felt and because of the perceptions we placed upon these experiences.

It is time to change; it is time to clean house. It is time to change these early, weighty thoughts and clear them out. Get connected to them so you can experience resolution. Resolution is easy once you connect to the memory. As you return to these memories now, you have the perspective of a mature mind and years of life experiences, so resolution is easy.

One of my early childhood experiences that I was able to connect to and bring into resolution occurred when I was about three or four years old. I wanted to do something to show my mother that I loved her. So I decided to draw for her a big, pretty picture on the wall. She became very angry with me, and from that experience I made the decision to never draw again. It was painful—a misconception. At age three or four, I made the decision to never draw even though this was one of my natural gifts and talents. This artistic ability has shown up in other areas throughout my life, but my desire to be a portrait artist lay dormant and was never acted upon until the day I connected to this memory. I knew I had a gift, but I didn't know I had turned it off because of this weighty, painful experience.

As an adult, I have the wisdom and experience to know why my mother was angry with me. The wall was not the artistic medium to use to express my gift or my love. This painful misconception changed the course of my life for years. Now I have resolution, and it is my choice whether I pick up the pencil to draw. I know the gift is within.

When you connect to your early memories and bring them into resolution by providing the time and place, you can create a totally different experience for your life. I am now free to express myself in this joyful fashion, and it brings me great joy to see my children develop their artistic talents. They all have them and are actively engaged in acting upon them. I see this gift in them and rejoice.

We are all here on the planet to learn, grow, and progress. We are here to experience opposition and to move forward in this experience. We each have great gifts and talents that are buried under our thick walls of protection, low-vibration memories, and old thoughts. Take the time to clear your thoughts, to bring them into resolution, to reframe them, and to have joy. Life keeps happening, but it doesn't need to be like it has been. It can be a joyful experience as you learn these new skills to help you successfully navigate through life.

Clear out the cobwebs of your past. Wipe clean the destructive memories and start anew. Begin your rebirth process with a clean mind and a pure heart, free of past illusions, mistakes, or misconceptions. Begin each new day as a new day, free of the weight and pain of your past. Raise your vibration by clearing out all those low-vibration experiences that are frozen in time. It is just perception, just energy; with just a thought, you can

change it! You can change it all. Just stick with me and I will
show you the way.

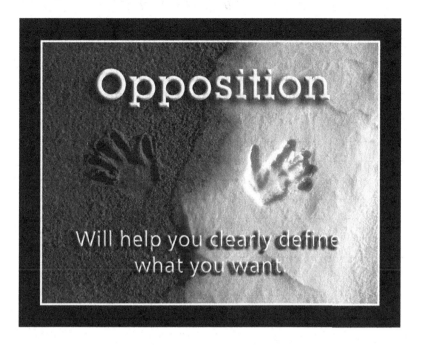

Changing Your Life
by Changing Your Thoughts

Practice

Review your life. Identify an area in which you feel stuck. Look for patterns or thoughts that keep repeating themselves. Record this information below.

_____
_____
_____
_____
_____
_____
_____
_____
_____
_____
_____
_____
_____
_____
_____
_____
_____
_____
_____
_____
_____
_____
_____
_____
_____
_____
_____
_____
_____

4

Raising Your Vibration to a High Joy State

Energy Work or Vibration Consciousness—What Is It?

Everything vibrates in its own rhythm and time at its own calibrated vibration. Everything in existence can be broken down into molecules, particles, and subatomic particles, which are all in motion. Even rocks, though they appear stationary to the naked eye, are actually in motion. If you were to take a particle of a rock and view it under an electron microscope, you would see its tiny particles in motion. Everything is in motion, even your family in front of the TV.

God is also in motion. His vibration is the highest vibration, and it is this vibration we are seeking to emulate. It is His vibration to which we are longing to return. This is our heritage as children of God. God vibrates in a high joy state, which is what I am in part trying to teach you how to achieve in a step-by-step process.

In *Webster's New World Dictionary college 4th edition*, the word *exalt* is defined as, "1. Rise on high, to elevate, to lift up." *Exaltation* means, "1. A feeling of great or excessive joy." This is our goal—to raise our vibrations to those of our Father in Heaven; to raise our vibration to His high joy state.

Returning to God Is the Purpose of Our Existence

We came to earth to receive a body and gain experience in a lower vibration sphere, to experience opposition, to feel what it is like to be in this earthly estate or this vibration. We came here to learn, to grow, and to then return home.

Part of our earthly experience includes an opportunity to use our agency, which is an opportunity to determine whether we would again choose to live as we did in the heavens—in oneness, in love, and in a high joy vibrational state. We are not left alone in this. Father in Heaven set up a system within our bodies to facilitate our return if we would attune ourselves to it. This system is intended to be used on a daily basis to help and guide us.

The system we each have within is a system of light. Everyone has it. This system is a light sensor that helps us recognize the vibrations of all things. This light sensor is known as the Light of Christ, or our conscience. Our light sensor helps us recognize the vibrations of things in and around us. Every person on the planet has one; no one is exempt. This is as much a part of you as the very earth your particles are derived from.

To understand energy further, let's first look at matter. Spiritual matter vibrates at a faster, higher frequency than earthly matter. When we, through the process of growth, education, and agency, raise our vibration to high-spirit frequencies, we are then able to operate within the higher spiritual laws, which govern the spiritual realm in a very natural way. For instance, in that high-spirit frequency, it would not be unnatural to walk on water, heal people, or turn water into wine. This was the frequency that Jesus Christ worked from, and this high-spirit frequency is what we are striving to emulate and achieve. The reason we are not experiencing these "miracles" in our lives is because we have not raised our vibrations to the frequency in which these experiences naturally occur.

We can have these miraculous experiences. They have been known to occur in people's lives, but they have been random and unintentional. It is my intention to teach you how to raise your vibration so that you may more powerfully draw upon these powers in an intentional, everyday manner.

This is a process and will take time, but becoming aware of the possibilities will facilitate your desire, enabling you to do the work that is required to achieve this joy-filled, high vibrational state.

The first step in raising your vibration is to get rid of what is keeping you weighed down and in pain. To accomplish this step, let's look at the magnificent power of your mind.

Are you aware of the power of your mind? Do you understand that your thoughts create your reality?

This is our starting point, this is where we will begin, and this is the first area we will work on to change. It is here, in the mind—both the conscious and subconscious mind—that we will let go of beliefs and thought patterns that aren't serving us, beliefs that are keeping us in a low vibrational state. You will work in this area for some time. If you want the end result of being like God, the master of the universe, this is where you begin. You first become the master of yourself, the master of your thoughts.

The first step in this process is to become aware of your thoughts. We think approximately sixty thousand thoughts a day.

What are you thinking? How are you using your thoughts? Are you spending them wisely?

Our thoughts, feelings, and beliefs are what create our reality. Look around—is there anything within your view that did not originate from thought? Everything you see came into being as a result of someone's contemplating the need for it. Our thoughts become things. If thoughts really create, what are you thinking, feeling, and believing? What are you creating? You can discover the answer to this question by looking at your life. Look at the results of all of your past thoughts; you are now living the results of your creation.

Are you creating and living the life of your dreams?

Building the Life of Your Dreams

If you were to set out to build a mansion, you would begin with the blueprint of a mansion. If you were to set out to build a shack, you wouldn't need blueprints. You would just start nailing boards together.

What are you building with your thoughts—a mansion or a shack?

Let's take a quick inventory. There are two work spaces on the following page. The first is "Mansion" and the second is "Shack." Let's begin by building a mansion with our thoughts. If you think shack thoughts, write them down as well, but first try intentional, mansion-building thoughts.

What do you want in your life? Have you ever thought about that? Some have been at this for a while, and some are just beginning. This is not a competition or a race. It is about building the best you, the best life you can.

What thoughts create or build what you want? What thoughts get in the way of creating what you want?

Write a quick, general outline of what you want in your life. If you think of things you don't want, write them in the Shack space. This exercise will be the beginning of becoming conscious of what you want and conscious of your thoughts. This information is to help you see clearly what you are creating and what you want to create. When you think of your mansion, this is the beginning of your blueprint or the beginning of how you want your life to turn out. Thoughts that are out of alignment with what you want are the results of unintentional creating— just hammering out your life and living out old memories, old patterns, and old habits. Is this what you want? Most of us don't intend to make a mess out of our lives. We all want something more. So let's begin by getting a very clear picture of what you do want in your mansion. (There is an extended work space for all the practice exercises in the Journey to Joy a Course About Living and Being in Joy Workbook.)

MY LIFE

Mansion

_____
_____
_____
_____
_____
_____
_____
_____
_____
_____
_____
_____

Shack

_____
_____
_____
_____
_____
_____

Energy work or vibration consciousness

Energy work or vibration consciousness in part is the work of becoming conscious of your thoughts, changing your thoughts, and stepping into new thoughts.

Not only do we vibrate at a certain frequency, but our thoughts also have a vibrational frequency. Thought is matter. Remember, everything you now see in physical form began first as a thought.

Our Internal Vibration Sensor

Becoming aware of your thoughts and what frequency they vibrate at is a significant part of your journey to joy. But how do we know the vibrational frequency of our thoughts?

This is where the internal light sensor comes in to play. Our light sensors operate in the realm of feelings. When you are thinking positive, mansion-building thoughts, you will feel feelings of joy because this is your heritage as a child of God. We are to live in a mansion, to be exalted, and to be in joy. If you think lower vibrational thoughts—thoughts that do not serve or build or that are out of alignment with what you really want—you will feel negative emotions. This is merely information from your light sensor, warning you that what you are now about, what you are thinking, is of a lower vibration and out of harmony with what you want.

Our thoughts fire so quickly that we need a back-up system to help us. So our feelings can give us messages at the same time we are thinking and speaking.

In the past, while involved in joyful activities, I would catch myself feeling down. I would then turn my thoughts to something more in alignment with what I wanted, and as a result I would instantly shift my feelings and be back in joy.

I remember one of my earliest experiences with becoming very conscious of this guidance system at work in my life. I had been to a doctor's appointment, and my husband had just picked me up for our return trip home. Just prior to leaving the doctor's office, I happened to weigh myself. This was always a sensitive subject because I have spent the greater portion of my life being overweight. When my husband picked me up, I felt fine, but then as we drove away I began to ponder this situation. I conceived a thought that was so out of harmony with what I really wanted for my experience that I instantly began to cry. My husband at that moment happened to look over at me and, seeing the tears sliding down my face, said in a concerned voice, "Tannie, what is the matter? What happened?" I knew instantly that the thought I had just entertained was out of harmony with what I wanted, and I quickly said, "Nothing is the matter. I just thought a negative thought, and I am going to change it right now." I instantly changed it to a thought that was more in harmony with my desires, and I felt happy. That was an amazing experience because I stopped misery the minute it set foot in my door and quickly changed my feelings to feelings of joy. My husband just happened to catch me making the U-turn.

From that point on, I began to become very conscious of my thoughts and intentions, and from this experience, I was able to see how significantly I could affect the way I felt each day.

When we become very intentional about our health, relationships, and life and focus on what we really want with regard to them, then there is really nothing that can stand in the way of our joy and success.

Remember, though, that this is a process and will take time, which is why I entitled this course *Journey to Joy.* My intention is to help you become a master builder of your life and to help you learn how to live and be in joy.

Family Patterns

When you start becoming conscious of your thoughts, you will begin a marvelous journey. You will not only become aware of your thoughts, but you will become aware of the enormous influence your family has had on your life. We not only inherit the physical characteristics of our ancestors; we also inherit their thought tendencies, thought patterns, and beliefs. You will discover these patterns as you travel. You will discover that these thought patterns didn't serve them any better than they are serving you. But understanding this and knowing that these family thought patterns exist gives you the power to change them.

In a CD series titled *From All Eternity* by Dr. John Lund, he spoke of a family of five siblings who were in the process of divorcing their spouses all at the same time. One of them thought that maybe there was a family communication problem and called Dr. Lund for help.

Dr. Lund spent time with the family and very quickly zeroed in on the communication problem. In a nutshell, they all held the limited belief of, "If I have to ask for it, it doesn't mean as much," and so no one asked for anything. They only *expected.* That belief was definitely a time bomb waiting to go off, and it did all at the same time for this family. We all have thought patterns that are not serving us. As we journey together, you will become aware of family patterns that are affecting your life in negative ways. As you pay closer attention to your life, they will begin to really pop out at you. It all begins with a desire to see and change them. I have often asked myself the questions, *Why do I feel this way?* or *Why do I do what I do?*

I have discovered a wealth of information by asking questions, and as a result my life has significantly changed for the better.

The first significant family pattern I connected to surfaced right after my eldest daughter gave birth to my first grandchild. The first time I took my younger children, who were living at home, to see our new baby girl, everyone was very excited to see her—that is, everyone except me. I felt I did not want to have anything to do with this new baby. I questioned my feelings. I thought, *This is strange. I just adore the baby across the street, and my own grandchild I have no interest in? What is this about? Where are these feeling coming from? I really want to know.*

I soon discovered the family pattern. In my father's family, it was common for the grandparents to raise the grandchildren. So in his family, a grandchild was not a welcomed, wonderful gift. It was a burden, another responsibility, another mouth to feed. As soon as I recognized and resolved the pattern, the feeling left and I could lovingly be around my sweet grandbaby without the baggage of this pattern pulling at me to avoid what I really loved.

Later I discovered another significant roadblock to joy. I had a pattern running that I was quite oblivious to for some time. It manifested in my outward behavior whenever I had a project or job to do around the house. I felt driven to keep at it until the job was complete. For instance, I would have to clean the entire house before we left for a vacation. When we worked in the backyard, I would push myself and my family to keep going long past wisdom and well into exhaustion. It used to drive my family crazy. I would work so hard that I could barely walk or move. Then when I was barely moving, I felt it was okay to stop because I was sick. This pattern went on for years. Then one day I found the core memory that this pattern was connected to.

It was an experience I had when I was about eight years old. My mother was a very hard-working woman, raising a family of five children ages eight to seventeen, of which I was the youngest. In order to do all she had to do to keep the family going, she would stay up into the wee hours of the night working, mostly to sew our clothes. She made most of our clothes by hand. One particular evening, Mother was planning an all-nighter, but this time it included the children. She was going to paint the house. I was exhausted; I just wanted to go to bed. It was at this time that my programming for this pattern was set in. Mom said, "You can't stop until the job is done." That saying froze in my belief system as truth, and so when I reached the tired or exhausted state, the program in my subconscious would click on "play" and I would have to keep going, unable to stop and never knowing why.

Boy, when I found that subconscious belief, what a joyful day it was! I could stop with the house half-done or the laundry half-done. I could even leave the floor half-swept. It was wonderful. You see, when your chosen profession is to be a mother, the job is never done. My belief clicked on "play" when I was tired and played out the entire program of, "You can't stop until the job is done." The job of being a mother was never done, so I could never stop. Therefore, to sustain that belief, I ran my health into the ground. The only way I would stop was by force, when my body would not move another inch, or when I would end up in bed, too sick to go on.

Do you have any unhealthy patterns in your life that you would really like to put the brakes on? Think for a moment. Do you have any behavior patterns you just don't get? Spend the next few minutes pondering this question. Think of the things you do that you just don't understand and wish you didn't do.

Pause for a moment and quickly scan your life. What are you doing that you don't understand? What would you like to change but have been unable to up to this point? What would you like to do but have felt for some reason that you couldn't? Once you have a few behaviors you don't understand or can't change written down, we will continue.

Behaviors I would like to understand and change, or family patterns I would like to put the brakes on:

_____

_____

_____

_____

_____

_____

_____

_____

_____

_____

_____

_____

_____

_____

_____

_____

_____

Good. Now that you have identified a few behaviors, what do you do with this information?

The logical thing is to change them, which is our intention. But before you can change things, you must first become aware that they exist. The family Dr. Lund assisted knew there was a problem because of the results in their lives, but they did not know the core or cause, so they called him for assistance.

Sometimes we need assistance to find the foundational problems to our mansion-building process. It is okay to ask for assistance. This is not a sign of weakness; it is a sign of strength. Think—you are building a mansion. Are there any elements of this process that you can't do yourself? You bet. There are many areas that you will need help with.

Mansion-Building Help Hotline

In my mansion-building process, I discovered a great resource. This is a twenty-four hour, seven-day-a-week service. You can ask anything you want about any subject you want, and you will get the most heavenly assistance. Here is the number to call: 1-800-Ask God. Yes, it's prayer.

If we were to call a contractor, we would not get what we needed from the contractor unless we told him exactly what our needs were and exactly what we wanted, right? Well, God works the same way. He needs to be asked. He needs to know exactly what you want. If you need help getting rid of patterns or tracing negative thoughts, pray and ask him to help you. He will direct your path every step of the way. All you have to do is ask. This is what I did, and I embarked on a marvelous journey of discovery.

Building a Mansion at Work: a Personal Experience

One of the students in the first class I presented this information to took this challenge to the office. She asked a coworker, "If you built a home with your spoken words and thoughts, what would you be living in now—a mansion or a shack?"

After some thought and discussion, they decided to become very conscious about what they were saying and how they said it. When one of them would say something like, "Oh, man. Life is the pits" or "I am so tired," the other one would ask, "Is that what you want to build? Is that what you want in your life?" Then they would quickly correct the statement or reframe it by saying the opposite or by saying what they wanted instead, like, "Isn't life great? I love having all this energy. I am so happy."

They had fun with it, and their lives really started to improve at the office and at home. They became very intentional about their lives and focused on great mansion-building thoughts.

Raising Your Vibration to a High Joy State

Practice

This week, begin to record in your Journey to Joy workbook the thoughts you have that are not mansion-building thoughts. Remember to use the cool little tool I mentioned in the beginning of this section—your vibration sensor.

Pay attention to your feelings. This is where it begins. When you find yourself feeling lower vibration feelings or frequencies, think, "What am I now thinking that is contributing to this low vibration state?" It is always there. If you are feeling down, depressed, or sad, then you are thinking down, depressing, or sad thoughts. Remember that this process will take time to master, but of course becoming a master builder would take time.

Our thoughts cause our feelings. When we think lower vibrational thoughts, we feel the feelings that accompany these thoughts. Our goal is to become conscious of our feelings and alter our thoughts so that we can be the master builders of our lives and live our lives in joy.

Jesus Christ was a master in this area. In fact, He was a master in all areas of His life; His desires were in alignment with His purpose. He was one with God, which is why He was able to function in the capacity of the high spirit frequencies and accomplish all He did. He also descended below, meaning He took on all the low vibration experiences as well. But throughout His life, He was always a master.

Our goal is to become the master craftsmen of our lives, to become a master creator like our Father in Heaven and His divine son, Jesus Christ.

Now it is your turn. Go for it! Build the life of your dreams!

5

Opposition and Family Life: Using Negative Experiences in a Positive Way

The most significant opposition we experience is within the family unit. Can this potent opposition actually facilitate our journey to joy?

It is possible. Our intention today is to learn how to turn these experiences into positive ones, thus changing our opposition into the gift of growth it was intended to be.

Think for a moment. What is the upside of being down? Is there any good that can come from a bad experience? How does opposition serve you? Have you ever had a positive outcome from a huge trial or bad experience?

Take a moment to think about these questions and record your thoughts below.

How Opposition Serves

_____

_____

_____

Here are a few other possibilities to consider and add to your list.

Opposition serves me by making me strong.

It teaches me what not to do.

It draws me closer to God.

I learn a lot about myself.

When I go through really hard things, I appreciate what others have sacrificed for me or have gone through themselves.

It provides opportunities to choose; I can choose life or death. I can forgive and love, or I can hate and be miserable.

I learn very clearly what I don't want.

It helps me to learn how to empathize.

It moves us into gratitude.

Now think of your personal experiences in opposition. What are some of the most trying experiences you have had or perhaps are now having in your family unit or within your close personal relationships? Record your thoughts below or in your student workbook.

My Personal Experiences

_____
_____
_____
_____
_____
_____
_____
_____
_____
_____
_____
_____
_____
_____

Other typical family problems might include these:
Whining children
Sibling rivalry
Money problems
Fighting and anger issues
Infidelity
Non- or miscommunication
Workaholism
Health issues
Selfishness, dishonesty
Mental illness
Drug addiction and alcoholism
Abuse
Jealousy
Power and control issues
Employment issues
Stress

Now that we have a great working list of opposition experiences, let's go back to one of the earlier questions. How can these experiences serve you? Think about your own situations first.

This is a great activity to do with a companion or friend because outsiders can offer a unique and different perspective about the problem. Try asking them this simple question: "Here is a problem." (State the problem.) "Can you tell me something positive that can come from this problem or situation?"

Focus on one particular problem at a time. Ask as many different people as you can this question and record the results. Getting a new and different perspective from those not involved in the problem is very helpful. Ask the most positive, upbeat people you know.

Why Opposition? A New Perspective from the Beginning

In the beginning, we lived in heaven with our Heavenly Father. We accepted His plan to come to earth to receive a body and experience life here. Part of this experience included having the veil of forgetfulness draped over our minds so that we could have experiences based on our earthly sojourn instead of our heavenly one. We all agreed. If we did not fully agree with the entire plan, we would not be here.

We came to earth for a very specific purpose. This purpose was to gain a physical body like our heavenly parents' so we could progress and grow to be like them and to experience opposition. There were other reasons as well: part of our intention for our experience here is to discover them all.

When we chose to come, we knew part of the plan was to experience opposition in the physical body. We were coming to our "Earth School of Opposition" to experience the opposite of all things.

By now, we have all had a really good dose of opposition. Look at the list again.

Whining children
Sibling rivalry
Money problems
Fighting and anger issues
Infidelity
Non- or miscommunication
Workaholism
Health issues
Selfishness, dishonesty
Mental illness
Drug addiction and alcoholism
Abuse
Jealousy
Power and control issues
Employment issues
Stress

I'd like to commend you on the great job you are doing. If this is schooling in opposition, we should all get an A+. So, then, if we are doing what we came here to do, why are we all moaning and complaining about it?

We all agreed to this experience or we would not be here. If we are here to experience opposition, you know and have pondered your version of it or perhaps some of your experiences in it. Then shouldn't we be rejoicing in the fact that we are doing what we came to do?

If you were to go to Harvard Law School to study and experience law, wouldn't that be a positive thing? It may be challenging and you might have to put some effort into completing your courses, but you would have the goal in mind and diligently work toward graduation. This is similar to our experience here on earth. We are here to experience the opposite of our heavenly home—to learn, grow, and make choices. When we complete our course and graduate, we can then return back to our heavenly home.

As with higher education, some attending this Earth School of Opposition will graduate with honors. Some will feel that they are barely making it, and some will feel that they are never going to get through it; they just want to quit and go home now. But this last choice is not an option, although sometimes it is an easy one to consider. We did not come to school to fail. We came to complete the course and return home to the Father with highest distinctions.

So here you are in this school and really getting a great dose of what you came here to experience. So what is the problem? Is there anything we can do to make it through all the tests and all these opposing classes and lessons we signed up for?

There certainly is! It is my firm belief that we are experiencing exactly what we signed up for. You see, if agency is an eternal law, then we had agency in our pre-earth lives as well. We had the opportunity to choose what we wanted to experience in this life. I am quite sure that we had a very clear course description and some really great advisors to assist us, including our Father in Heaven.

So now we are in school, going through the courses we signed up for. Do you intend to make it through school with honors?

For the dedicated students, the only way to finish the course is to keep your focus and realize that you are right on track. You are here doing the very things you came to do, and you are doing a great job experiencing opposition in the physical body. The only thing we have working against us is our attitudes about our course.

You can graduate with honors and make it through this school of opposition in joy when
- You realize you are doing the very thing you came to do and that you have done a great job at it.

- You stop beating yourself up and stop thinking you have done something wrong because your course is tough.
- You see that you are making it and that you have done the best you could do.
- You realize that you are not alone in this and have a 24-7 student support and advisory team working for you and with you.
- You can actually feel—and I want to emphasize the word *feel*—that you are not alone and have already learned so much. Then you will be able to go through this school of opposition in joy.

Remember in high school or college when you worked really hard studying for a test and you got the grade you were working for? Remember how that felt? You were so relieved and so happy. Get into the energy of doing well on a test. See yourself making it, and you will.

If you could wake up each day and say, "I am doing great in school," and change your attitude about your course work and your experiences, you would feel and experience an increased measure of joy. This attitude may be new to you, and it may take some time to slip into, but you can do it. If you catch yourself wearing the old "beat yourself up" outfit or attitude from your old school of thought, quickly take it off and put on your suit for success. If you do this, you will graduate with honors and journey through life in joy.

The Language of Success 101

Now imagine that you are in a class called The Language of Success 101. What do you imagine the course work would be? Let's compose a list.

This 101 class would be all about success. I imagine we would write and orate something like this: "I am doing remarkable.

Look at all the great lessons I have learned! I have learned so much from my experience. I have a great list of things I will never choose again. I am making it. I am successful."

How do you know a choice is bad unless you make it, trust a loved one who has made it, or believe God when he offers you a "Thou shalt not"? We learn by our experiences.

We have been blessed with great schooling resources— our internal guidance system, for one, and a fine how-to book (the Scriptures). If we use these resources daily, we will save ourselves a lot of pain.

Sometimes we follow our guidance systems and sometimes we choose to go the long way, but, you know what? You learn from both. It is all perfect.

How to Have Joy in Opposition

To have joy in opposition, the first step is to always be kind and loving to yourself. If you ever speak negatively about yourself, like, "I'm so stupid" or "I can't do anything right," that will take you down quite a few notches on the joy meter. You will never have joy in the absence of self-love.

Next, look at your opposition with new eyes of understanding. As soon as you become aware of the trial, struggles, or pain, begin to look for the lesson or the good in that situation. Every experience we have has a lesson attached. There is always something to learn. If you get the lesson right away, guess what? You pass the course, and the teacher, or the opposition, will disappear.

If you are in a trial and have been in it for a very long time, you are missing the lesson somewhere. Ask for help. Ask, "What am I supposed to learn from this? I am ready to get the lesson and move on. I am really tired of this course." When our teachers' jobs are complete, then we don't need the teachers anymore. We have got it. We have learned what they are here to teach us.

The final and crowning glory of each lesson is gratitude. When you are grateful for the lessons, for the opposition, and for the growth experienced and you express the gratitude you feel inside, you will be in joy. This act of gratitude must be sincere, for God knows the thoughts and intentions of your heart. You don't get to graduate until you complete the process. Again, the final step is to be grateful for the very thing that caused you the most growth.

Look back on one of your hardest, most difficult trials. What have you learned from that experience?

This is the type of thinking that will move you out of misery and pain and into joy. You are here doing a great job! Learn from your trials and move past them. Quit beating yourself up for doing what you came here to do, for doing what you planned on doing in the beginning.

Remember The **Sun** is always shining behind the clouds.

Opposition and Family Life: Using Negative Experiences in a Positive Way

Practice

Are you ready to move forward with the next step? Good. Let's begin by looking at the biggest trial of your life or a significant trial that you are now facing. Write a long list of what you have learned from this experience. Write a positive list, in the absence of bitterness. If bitterness is present, you still have a ways to go.

If you are feeling bitter, you may need to use your release techniques until the bitterness is gone and you are back in a balanced state of being. (Release techniques are found in Chapters 16 and 17.) It's okay if you have to work on it for a few days. It is better to work on it for a while than to keep it in. Bitterness is a very low vibration with a big negative charge. If, after a few days of working on it, you still feel out of sorts, you might consider getting help. It is okay to get help when you find something with a lot of punch.

When writing your list, look for the positive in your negative life situation or trial. Look for everything you have learned.

Refer to Leah's Lesson in Chapter 34, and Simple Techniques to Raise Your Vibration in Chapter 8. These chapters will give you an idea of what I am suggesting here. At the end of Chapter 8, there is a list of positive affirmations intended to help you move into gratitude for your life's greatest lessons.

If you need help with this practice exercise, again go to a close friend or loved one and consider saying the following: "Here is the problem." (State the problem.) "Now can you tell me something positive that can come from this experience?"

Focus on one particular problem and ask this question to as many different people as you can and record the results. This exercise will greatly assist you on your journey to joy.

What have I learned from my greatest trials?

_____
_____
_____
_____
_____
_____
_____
_____
_____
_____
_____
_____

Learning to See Opposition as a Gift

I am thankful for my kids' messy rooms because it is an indication that they are learning through trial and error the importance of order. They, through their own mistakes, discover that when we put things in their place, we find them. How many tries will it take us?

I am thankful for a sink full of dirty dishes because it provides an opportunity of service. When it is my kids' turn, the dishes are piling up, and they are very busy, I can do the dishes and through my actions say, "Here, let me help you," modeling what I want them to do for others.

I am thankful for my hot house in the summertime. When it is hot, it is because a lot of friends are over or someone is in the kitchen cooking, both a great blessing.

I am grateful for a house full of company. This experience helps me appreciate my quiet, alone times more.

I am grateful for a husband who is often at work because his actions say, "I am doing this so you can be at home with our children to love them, teach them, and be there for them when they are in need."

I am grateful for the pain I have felt in my life. It has been a strong, moving, motivating force. I have learned a great deal from the experiences.

I am grateful for experiencing lack; it has given me understanding and compassion for those in need. I have also experienced creating beauty having very little to work with. For example, our first Christmas tree was decorated with dried weeds that looked like baby's breath and ribbons. It was beautiful.

I am grateful for obesity; it has taught me a great deal. I have learned compassion for those who struggle, a lot about nutrition, and the fact that diets really don't work because you are focusing on your imperfections—what you don't like about yourself or don't want—not your perfection and what you do want. And most significantly, it has kept me close to God.

I am grateful for sibling rivalry. It has taught me about my inner battles. Each time my children fight, I ask myself, *What is this teaching me about me?* The answer is always there.

I am grateful for my inner guidance system; it is such a significant part of my life. It has guided me throughout my life.

I am grateful for everything that bugs me. It is an indication of something inside of me. When I see something on the outside I do not like, I go inside to find it and change it. Then it is no longer present in my experience. The spirit told me once, "We live in a reflective universe." It is true. Everything you see is a reflection of something in you.

I am grateful for a husband who never complains when I don't do what he expects because he knows in his heart I am doing the best I can.

I am grateful for a husband who would always buy our kids fun things with "money we don't have." He married a wife who could never afford them because she was always on a budget. He made the kids really happy, and we never missed the money. I have since learned to rejoice in the gift of his generosity and to try to be more like him, focusing on our abundance instead of our lack.

I am grateful that teenagers have to have a driving permit and drive with an adult first. This has given me great talk time with my children.

I am grateful for my son. He has taught me so much about love, laughter, tolerance, and what it is like to be a boy, something I never got to experience.

I am grateful for all the political mail and calls I receive because they are a wonderful reminder that I have a voice and that I can use it to make a difference. They also remind me that I live in a country where we are free to say what we want. We are free to choose. I love America!

I am grateful each time I do my laundry. It reminds me of how blessed I am to live in the day of washers, dryers and disposable diapers. I then think of all of the other conveniences I enjoy, like a wonderful hot shower on cold mornings, lights that don't stink like a burnt match or kerosene when you turn them on, music that comes out of a tiny box, my blessed computer, and, the most wonderful of all gifts, the phone! I can talk to my kids who live so far away. I love my life!

I am grateful for all the times I have spent with sick or grouchy children because it was a time to say thank you for teaching me patience and tolerance and all of the other virtues I have needed to become like my heavenly parents.

Look at your opposition and begin to see the gifts. They are there, hidden in the midst of darkness. When you see them, light begins to shine from within and you will feel joy.

Affirmations

Making the Most Out of My Opposition

Positive affirmations are a great tool to help you turn a negative life situation into positive one. If you breathe deeply and relax as you read or experience these from the CD, it will help take these affirmations to a deeper level of consciousness.

I am learning from my mistakes. All parts of my experiences are important. I am connected to my life's purpose, and I am secure, confident, and moving forward in that purpose. I am enjoying growing and changing. I am taking good care of myself. I am using negative energy and experiences in a positive way. Taking time out for me is really important; I love the way it feels. I am compassionate, patient, loving, and accepting of others, all because of the outcome of my experiences in opposition. Opposition has been a great teacher, but now I am choosing to learn in joy.

I am getting it! Life is easy, fun, and playful. Look at all of the great experiences I have had. I am a different person now. The new me is alive and well and strong. I am learning the lessons and moving forward in joy. I am fulfilling my life's purpose. I am full of life and hope. I am powerful. I am making a difference, and I am strong. My life's purposes are being realized. Look at that—so much good has come from all this. Look at the rainbow; it has never looked so bright.

I'm seeing the good in all things. My life is like a fine work of art. It is the contrast of light and dark that creates beautiful pictures, and I can see that in my life as well. I am moving forward in grace and ease. I am living the life I always dreamed of. I am gifted and talented. Look how strong I have become. I am a builder of all that is good. My life just keeps getting better. I am filled with hope and joy. God knows me and honors my efforts. God loves me and supports me and is always there to hear and answer my prayers. I never dreamed that going through these experiences could teach me so much wisdom and love.

I am joyfully alive. I am grateful for my life's experiences. I am alive in hope for a wonderful future. My family is safe and taken care of. I am remembering my life. My life is filled with love, hope, joy, and gratitude. I am safe and secure; I am healthy and filled with love. I am finding solutions to my problems; the answers just flow in. Bad hair today—fashion trend tomorrow. I know who I am, and I love being me. When my life gets out of hand, I simply place my hand in God's and we are back in the flow. Life is filled with meaning and purpose.

I am moving on. I am moving forward and helping others feel the joy life has to offer. I am a great strength. I am creating a joyful future. I am creating a new life filled with abundance, prosperity, and financial freedom. I am abundantly blessed; there is no end to my joy. I am fulfilled and delighted in my new life. My heart is whole and complete. I trust my life's divine purpose. My energy is always moving in a forward pattern. I am open and flowing. I am inhaling the future and exhaling the past. It is so easy to let go.

I now live for a higher purpose. I have raised my vibration through gratitude and unconditional love. I respect boundaries, my own and others'. I accept and allow others' reactions. I embrace all of my life's lessons; I do my best and leave the rest to God. Small steps are great; I am still moving forward. I can see clearly now. I have a great attitude. Staying calm really works for me. I am grateful for the gift of life. I am happy to be here. I am more than my experience. I am my pure essence. I am divine, I am complete, and I am a child of God.

6

Discovering What You Want and Learning How to Stay on Course

Not far away
in the Sunshine
another
Perfect day
is waiting

Tannie Bennett

Amy Beck

Your Perfect Day

Today we are going to learn how to get from where we are now to where we want to be, which for our course intention is in a constant state of joy.

To begin, let's review where we are. What's happening in your life on a daily basis? Quickly scan your typical day. This is a mental scan; you will not need to write anything down yet. Start with the moment you first wake up. What are your routines?

Now that you have your daily routines in mind, do you realize how many patterns you just identified? There was an entire day's worth. Why did I have you scan your day? To point out that your day is filled with patterns. If every day is filled with these types of patterns, are you ever going to get where you want to go?

Think again—where do you want to go? What do you want to experience? We have worked a bit on this with our mansion- and shack-building exercise and at other times during this course. Now let's get a very clear picture of just exactly what you want.

What do you want to experience in your life?

What experiences do you want to have on a daily basis?

What do you want to achieve, and what do you want to feel each day?

It is very important to have a clear picture of this in your mind because if you do not know where you are going, you will never get there.

If your day is filled with patterns you are not even aware of, you will continue to experience a random life with no specific intentions and no specific destination. Can you imagine going on a vacation without a single destination or plan? Imagine how your vacation would turn out.

Now imagine a vacation in which you planned for months or even years, and you had every detail arranged. What a powerful experience that would be.

Do we give our lives as much thought as we do our vacations?

If we don't plan our fun and joy and if we are not intentional about it, it will never happen on a regular basis. We may have a random amount of joy, but if you want to have a joy-filled life, you will become very intentional about your life.

Now that you have identified some of your patterns, take the next few minutes to identify what you want in your life. Be very specific. List your ideas on a separate piece of paper or in your workbooks.

As you are compiling your list, keep in mind your well-thought-out vacation. Plan your life as you would a wonderful vacation. Details are very important!

Remember—details, details, details!

What I Want in Life

_____
_____
_____
_____
_____
_____
_____
_____
_____
_____
_____
_____
_____

Now that you have some idea of what you want, let us look at a day filled with it. We are going to create a perfect day.

It is best to work with a partner on this. When you team up, tell your partner your idea of a perfect day. You will want to take your time on this one because details are important. Take at least ten minutes, or more if you can, to share your idea of a perfect day. Then, listen to your partner's perfect day. As the listening partner, your job is to just listen and give an occasional "Oooo, ahhh" and smile appropriately. You can glean wonderful ideas from your partner, ideas that you may never have considered before.

The first time I did this exercise, I was traveling with my niece Jenilyn. It was a wonderful experience. I asked Jeni to describe her perfect day. Jeni became so descriptive in her perfect day that it was as if I were right there with her. I was surprised when I found myself mentally running up a mountain with Jeni because I loved the way this experience felt in my body. That idea was something I had never even considered before—to love running up a mountain? In my past experience, that spelled pain. So it was a new thing for me to run up a mountain and love it, to love the way it made my body feel. She then took me mentally to Sedona, Arizona, which is very close to where I grew up. I could vividly remember the smell of the sycamore trees in the summer and hear the creek as it gurgled along its path. She bought a sweet caramel apple from a little Sedona shop and vividly described the taste, another experience that was new to a perfect day. It was wonderful. Jeni opened up new ideas and helped me get beyond my present thinking. She gave me something new to consider, something new to experience.

We are so stuck in our patterns of thinking that it is tricky to change and get into another frame of mind.

Creating your perfect day is a time to dream, a time to learn, a time to let yourself go. Go to the far reaches of the world if you like; this will be a joyous time.

I remember another perfect day creation experience. I was with my husband on our Friday night date. It had been a very busy week, and I had hardly had a chance to talk to him. As we drove toward our destination, I started talking to him about our finances. In times past, this had always been a big trigger subject for us, but I figured we had grown so much that we could handle it. Well, I learned from this experience that we still had some growing to do. The results were not joyful. I quickly changed the subject.

On the way home, I said, "Okay, honey, I am going to give you two subjects, and whatever you say about them, keep it positive, okay?" He agreed to try. I said, "Friday night dates and money." He took this challenge and ran with it. It was a most enjoyable experience. This alone was a perfect moment. He created the most wonderful date nights I could possibly imagine. He is an artist not only with his pen but also with his imagination. I was captivated by the experience. It was magnificent. By the time we were finished with our real date, I felt so in love with him. Dreaming and creating a perfect day is a perfect time to go into joy, a perfect time to expand your focus and step out of old patterns.

After this first experience with my husband, life just got better. We spent more time sharing our perfect days together. Then, as a surprise for our twenty-fifth wedding anniversary, he recreated mine. It was a day I will never forget.

As we travel through life, it is important to keep our focus on what we want and on where we want to go. Have you ever decided to go someplace—perhaps the store—only to become distracted and drive right past your destination? Then you stop yourself down the road and think, *Now, where am I going?* Our intention for this course is to focus again on where we want to go. We have lost our focus. We have become so focused on what we don't want that we have driven right into it. Think of the times you have taken your eyes off the road for a split second only to find yourself off the straight and narrow and heading in a direction you really didn't want to go. When you find yourself off, you then quickly correct your course. What if we did not correct our course? What kind of ride would we experience? A pretty bumpy one, I imagine, or maybe even a painful one.

Think about your life again. How are you doing? Are you on course, or are you experiencing the warning rivets of life? Does your life feel pretty unsettled at times? Do you feel like you're in the ditch or like you just did a face plant in the pavement? The warning signs, the pain, and the bumps are all wake-up calls telling you that a course correction is needed.

When your life is going smoothly, do you look at what you are doing to make it run like that? Do you question why it is going so well or draw your attention to what you are thinking? What are you now doing to experience this wonderful ride? Pay attention to what you are doing right so you can repeat the experience.

While driving, we will travel where our focus is. If your heart is focused on one thing and your mind is focused on something else, you will experience a pretty bumpy ride. We need to be of one heart and one mind. If your heart and mind are divided, you will never get to where you want to go. Remember, though, that wherever you travel and wherever you end up, you have valuable information. If you don't like where you are, you can change directions anytime you want. If you feel like you are pulling the steering wheel of your life, trying to keep your focus, and you still end up in the ditch, it is because of the division of your heart and mind.

How do you get your heart and mind working together? By clearing out what is at your core, at the heart of your being, by clearing your subconscious negative programming. Clear out these disharmonies, and then you can get to where you want to go in joy and peace.

In my early course experiences, I felt like I was trying to steer with all my might but someone else had a hand on the wheel. My life was going in a direction I did not want to go. But, you know, it was all perfect because from that very experience, I discovered so much about myself. I discovered my purpose, passions, and spiritual contracts. It was from that experience that I learned I needed to clear out the disharmonies within my heart so that I could live and be in joy and get to where I wanted to go.

Everything you learn about yourself is good. It is all information, and it will serve to help you move into your joy if you take the time and opportunity to do so.

In review, the most significant thing you can do is to clearly define what you want. Focus on it, and keep your focus on it. If you take your eyes off of what you want, you will end up with what you don't want.

Remember the story of Peter walking out upon the water to meet the Savior? As long as Peter kept his eyes on the Savior, he was able to walk on the water. When he took his eyes off of the Savior and looked at the storm, he began to sink. The Savior then rescued him, as He does us when we feel like we are sinking or have lost our focus. Keep your eyes on the Son and the shadows will fall behind. Keep your focus on where you want to go and what you want to experience in life, and it shall be.

Note: I invite you at this time to experience the imageries "Remember the Joy" and "Perfect Moments I and II" found on the second imagery CD.

These imageries are intended to help you find joy in life's simple pleasures. Having a repertoire of perfect moments in your mind will enable you to change your thought channel quickly, moving out of struggle and pain into joy. When you feel you are off the road, simply think of a perfect moment and move back into joy.

Begin creating your own perfect moments. When you find yourself loving what you are doing, simply frame it as a perfect moment. Focus on every element of the experience, and then cement the moment in your mind. Then, when you need an energy boost, think of your perfect moment long enough to shift into the feeling. And soon you will marvel at how perfectly wonderful your life is becoming.

My Perfect Moment

I remember one of my first framed perfect moments. My daughter, her husband, and her little baby girl were visiting. She and her husband had driven through the night and were very tired when they arrived at three o'clock in the morning. The baby woke up two hours later. Amy brought her into me and asked, "Mom, could you hold the baby so I can get more sleep?" "Sure, honey," I answered. "I would love to."

I snuggled her up in her little blanket and took her outside on the front swing so everyone else could go back to bed. It was a beautiful summer morning and gently raining outside. I remember holding the baby as she snuggled up against me. I remember the blanket she was wrapped in, the smell and sound of the rain, the leaves on the trees, the bird's song, and the gentle whisper of the wind. I remember the cool of the morning on my bare feet. I remember it all because I framed it: "This is a perfect moment." I wanted to remember every detail of that moment, and I have. I have returned to the memory many times, especially when I am missing my granddaughter. I hold her often in my mind. I enjoy loving her and being with her on the front swing of forever.

Since then I have framed many perfect moments, and I love returning to them any time. It has helped me to love and enjoy my family and not miss them so much when they are gone.

Love and joy are only a thought—a perfect moment—away.

Discovering What You Want and Learning How to Stay on Course

Practice

What do you want to experience in your life?
What experiences do you want to have on a daily basis?
What do you want to achieve?
What feelings do you want to feel each day?

It is very important to have a clear picture of this in your mind because if you do not know where you are going, you'll never get there.

Write the answer to the questions above, and write a very detailed description of what you want.

_____
_____
_____
_____
_____
_____
_____
_____
_____
_____
_____
_____
_____
_____
_____
_____
_____
_____
_____

69

A Positive Emotion Journal

Recording Your Perfect Moments

When you find things in your life that make you happy, life becomes joy filled. When you focus on your gifts, what you're grateful for, and what you love about your life, life can become truly magical. This is our goal; this is what fills our life with purpose. As you focus on these experiences and feelings, it is easy to stay on the road to joy. You can experience these feelings of peace and joy in anything you do. Notice what makes you feel happy and joy filled. Record these experiences so that when you are in negative energy, you can go to your positive journal and shift out of your negative feelings. It is the equivalent of changing your thought channel.

Keeping a positive emotion journal is very helpful. When you are in the act of reading or writing in your journal, in that moment of time you will be on the road to joy. You will be realigning yourself with what you want. Your positive, magnetic, vibrational attractor will be on. You will be announcing to the universe, "I am on course; I am ready to receive."

Your positive emotion journal will be a great place to record your perfect moments, your perfect days, and all the wonderful feelings you want to remember. It will be a place to record your wonderful memories and your special, sacred imagery experiences.

You may choose to call your positive emotion journal by another name, perhaps, "My Perfect Days," "My Gratitude Journal," "My Perfect Moments," "Evidence of My Perfectly Wonderful Life," "My Happy Thoughts," or "The Magic of My Life."

Your life is very important, and keeping a record of it is a great way to acknowledge this fact. Think of the great men and women of the past. Much has been written about them. Who better to record your life and how you feel about it than you? Experience the magic of your life; experience the magic of being you.

7

How to Get Answers to Life's Problems

At times, we feel that *life* and *stress* are synonymous. We feel stuck, angry, and frustrated. Life is just one big struggle, and we don't know where to turn to get the help we need. We pray for help; seek out professionals; and consult with clergymen, doctors, close family members and friends, but we still struggle with the same old problems. Then the struggle to get over the problem becomes part of the problem.

So what do we do? Think about this for a moment. What is the magic formula? What brings lasting change? We have worked on our problems for years, yet we seem to keep going down the same old road. What is the magic element that creates change? Is there a magic element? Think back on some of the biggest trials you have faced throughout your life. When you made the final move out of the trial, what was it that brought you to the point of change? What was the movement or action on your part? Have you ever thought about what moved you out? The answer is the same one that will move you out of the trials you are now facing.

My intention is to serve by teaching techniques that can provide lasting results, but this next technique may surprise you in its simplicity. I personally have had plenty of experience with this one. I know it works because I have done it over and over again. What is my secret formula for getting answers to my life's problems? What moved me forward? What was it that so significantly facilitated my movement into joy?

Well, the answer is pretty simple. It is prayer. I know you may have thought about this as a possible answer, and you have probably had experience with prayer. But do you have experience in getting answers to your prayers? Do you pray knowing that you will receive the answers you seek?

I am not talking about an occasional once-a-year type miracle. I am talking about an everyday occurrence. I am talking about going to God, asking a question, and getting it answered quickly—right on the spot, even before you close your prayer or very soon afterward. Have you had the experience of getting answers to your prayers right when you ask for them? Think about your prayer experiences. Think of all the times you have had your prayers answered.

Do you realize you can have such experiences? You can have a twenty-four-hour, seven-day-a-week online service with God if you want it. It is already yours; it's just that most of us aren't using this great service to the capacity that we could.

It is like having a beautiful car in the driveway and using only the horn. Each day we walk out to our shiny car, open the door, and honk the horn to call the kids home from around the neighborhood. Think of all the uses you have for your vehicles. We use them every day of our lives. But are we using the vehicle of prayer to its full capacity? Or are we just honking our horns, announcing to God, "I'm checking in! I am doing my duty. I'm calling home"? What a waste of a great vehicle.

Most of us have experienced prayer, and some are very proficient with this tool. Whatever your level of expertise is, I am here to encourage you to amp up your power with it.

How do you do this? Simply by having an intention to do so, by announcing to God and the universe, "I am having more effective prayers. I am getting my answers more clearly and frequently. I recognize these answers as they come to me, and I am fulfilled in my communications with God." As soon as you choose an intention and vocalize it, the magic begins. The more potent the feeling behind your intention is, the more powerful the answer experience will be.

I know some of you may feel a little uncomfortable with the announcement I just suggested. To some, it may sound as if I am demanding an answer from God. But if you recall, all miracles are accompanied with the pure knowledge that they will occur. This statement will be effective only if you believe God will honor your request.

Just last night, I read about a particular situation. I contemplated my experience with a similar situation, and I became very concerned. The more I thought about it, the more upset I became. I was pondering the possibility of being used by an acquaintance. Not liking what I was feeling, I took it to God and announced, "I need help." I said, "I do not like what I am feeling, and I want to know the truth in the matter. I want to know this individual's intentions. Were they honorable and pure?"

I knew the emotional state I was in was not creating a good energy in which to hear my answer, so I went to bed knowing I would soon receive the answer. I awoke several hours later and went into another room to contemplate the situation. Very quickly, I received the answer. I felt at peace knowing that my acquaintance's heart was pure and his intentions honorable. If I had received the opposite answer, I would have still been okay. I would have known there was a great lesson in this experience through which I would receive immense growth.

Part of hearing and receiving the answers we seek is being in a position to hear any answer we are given. Whatever answer we receive, it is important to be at peace and move forward in it.

Often we delay our own answers because we don't really want to hear what God has to say about the situation. We don't really want to know. Our heart is divided. We want help, but we have fear about what that help will look like when it shows up. So in essence, we really don't want to know.

Since God judges by the thoughts and intentions of our hearts, do you think he is going to give you an answer you don't really want? No, he won't. If you are not getting answers to your prayers, it is because you do not really want to hear what he will tell you. You have fear.

Fear is our greatest stumbling block in receiving the answers we seek. My fears kept me stuck and in pain for years because I was afraid Heavenly Father was going to tell me I had been wrong all my life and that life was not how I perceived it to be. So what happened? My incorrect perceptions about life became so big and so in my face that I finally turned to God and said, "Okay, I'm ready to listen. If I am wrong, it's okay because I just can't go any further like this. It is not worth it."

I gave up my fears, let go of my need to be right, and just submitted myself to Him. When I let go of the reins (my need to be right) and gave them to Him, I said, "Okay, God, I don't know how to fix this. What do I need to do?" Once I submitted myself totally to whatever the answer was and became determined that I was going to be okay with it, then the heavens opened, and step by step I got out of the mire. I got out of the pit I was in.

Let's review a few important steps in getting the help you need.

1. Desire is the first important step; we must first want heaven's help.
2. Next is petitioning God in prayer, asking for what we want and need. You see, God honors agency; He

will never interfere unless He is invited in. Have you asked for the help you need?

3. Set your intention to get the answers you need, and then pray in faith. Have your heart be one with Him, not divided. Do you really want to know the answer?

4. Pay attention to your fears. Do you have any regarding what God will tell you? Can you accept anything He tells you knowing it will be for your good and that He truly loves you and wants what is best for you?

5. Submit to the answers. Whatever comes in is going to be okay.

6. Act on the answers you receive. Move forward in faith.

There is a divine order of prayer, a pattern to use to help us when we pray. Do you know what the divine order is? It is really very simple.

1. First, you open your prayer in Heavenly Father's name. He has many names and titles. Use the one you are comfortable with. I open with "Dear Heavenly Father," or simply "Heavenly Father."

2. Next, we thank Him and acknowledge His hand in our life. You can use this time to express gratitude for all your gifts and blessings.

3. Then, ask for what you need and want, whatever it is.

4. Last, close in the name of His beloved son, Jesus Christ. I simply say, "In the name of Jesus Christ, Amen "

The greatest key in getting what we need from God is to first ask these questions:

- Do I really want to know the answer?
- Am I really ready for the answer?
- Am I ready to do as He suggests?

Our greatest stumbling block in getting answers is our fear. So if you are not getting daily answers to your prayers, this is where you look.

What do you do if you discover fear? How do you get your fears out of the way?

Before I answer these questions, I want to make something very clear. The first thing you will want to remember is to be kind and loving to yourself. Never beat yourself up for having fears or for not knowing something. We have a tendency to do that very easily, which is why I am giving this warning. Remember, we are here on this earth to gain experiences in opposition, in not knowing, in not having faith, and in not hearing God clearly. So in truth, *you are right on course.* You are experiencing the opposite of your truth. After we have had enough opposition and are soft and moldable, we turn to God and the magic begins.

Are you familiar with the Bible parable of the potter and the clay? The potter cannot mold clay that is crunchy, crusty, stiff, and hard. Our opposition is intentional; it softens us so we can be flexible and workable, providing the master potter the perfect medium to work with. Through the course of our opposition, we become soft and turn to God, and then He has something to work with. He sure can't mold us if we are stiff, fearful, and unwilling to do as He suggests.

So what do we do with our fears? Do you know?

You let them go. Fear is what is making you stiff and unmoldable.

Have you ever heard the expression "frozen in fear"? That is what fear does to us. It freezes us and keeps us stuck. We will never get where we want to go if fear is present.

Most of the fear we have operates at the subconscious level. You can bring it up to the surface if you want to. If you are particularly stuck in one area and don't know where the fear is, ask for it to be revealed to you. It will be. You will get it—that is, if you really want to know.

Sometimes our fear is so great that we need professional help to get through it. This is okay. Once you experience going through a few of those doors, you realize it's not so bad and are ready to clear all of your fears. Then you will find joy in the process of letting go and moving on, realizing the hard part was actually holding on to the fear and pain. It takes a lot of energy to hold that stuff in. No wonder we are exhausted.

Life is so wonderful! There are so many new adventures waiting. Discover what lies ahead. Get connected to the man in charge. Get connected to the one person who really knows all the answers and really knows just what you need in your life to heal. Connect to the God of miracles; connect to the power of eternal love.

How to Get Answers to Life's Problems

Example

I can't even begin to tell you a portion of my experiences in getting answers to my life's problems through prayer because I get them every day. I have experienced many miracles throughout my life because of prayer, such as the healing of my children when they were sick, finding money in my pocket when I really needed it, having someone stop with an extra tank of gas for my car five short minutes after I ran out and prayed for help, finding my glasses in the grass, and keeping my home out of foreclosure and my utilities on when I had no income for over a year. Yes, I have had many wonderful experiences throughout my life, but today I would like to share one of my personal favorites. I love this story not only because it is an example of the pure and simple prayer of a child but because of what it taught me about parenting.

God, Can I Have a Cookie?

Our family had just finished dinner one evening, and I stayed in the kitchen to clean up the table and put things away before we all retired to the living room for more family together time. I placed a warm plate of chocolate chip cookies on the table for our dessert. Just then, my four-year-old daughter Katie came bouncing into the kitchen. Seeing the cookies on the table, she asked, "Mommy, can I have a cookie?"

I answered, "No, Katie. You didn't finish your hamburger or your squash, and besides, the cookies are for family home evening."

She then placed her little hand on her hip and announced, "Well, you're not the boss of me."

I said, "Oh, really? Who is then?"

She answered confidently, "Heavenly Father."

Knowing God would back me on this one, I said, "Well, great then. Why don't you go ask Heavenly Father if you can have a cookie?"

She ran down the hall to her bedroom to pray. A few short minutes later, she came back with a mile-wide smile and announced, "Mommy, Heavenly Father said I could have a cookie."

I said, "Oh really? Why don't you tell me exactly what Heavenly Father said to you?"

She said, "Heavenly Father said that after I eat my hamburger and after I eat my squash and after family home evening, I can have a cookie."

I thought to myself, *Didn't I just say that?* Then I realized the difference—God said yes, and I had said no.

Wow. What a lesson in parenting and pure childlike faith.

When we ask anything of God in faith we always get what we want, even if it is a cookie.

How to Get Answers to Life's Problems

Practice

Find an area in your life where you feel stuck and identify the fear attached. Record your findings below.

Once you find the fear, it is easy to simply make a new choice and let the fear go. We feel fear when we lack understanding and knowledge of truth. When you are able to make the connection and really look at your fears, you will soon realize that your fears are unfounded. Then, making a new choice is easy. If for some reason you find it difficult to get beyond the fear, say your little prayer and ask that you might clear this fear and whatever it is attached to from the very core of your being. Then simply trust that your petition will be granted, and it will be so. (An example of this prayer is given on pages 172 and 173.)

8

Simple Techniques to Raise Your Vibration

I would like to draw your attention to a word in the title of this course. The word is *journey*. *Journey* refers to the elements of time and movement. The journey to joy is a day-to-day process. We will continue on this journey until we are able to maintain this happy, joy-filled, high vibrational state. If we don't arrive at our destination today, are we to get out of our metaphoric cars and beat ourselves into the pavement because we are not there? No. This is a process, a journey—one that we are to enjoy in its entirety. In fact, the process is what we will be learning so much from. Otherwise, our course might be called "Beam Me to Joy." Some of us might like that idea at this point, but this is not our intention, nor was it our Father in Heaven's when He sent us to earth to live and gain knowledge and experience. Your earthly life is an experience in time. Remember this and be kind to yourself as you learn how to stay on the road and make each day of your journey joy filled.

Setting Daily Intentions

An important technique or skill required for a successful journey is the practice of setting daily intentions. An intention is what you intend to experience or what you intend an event to be like. An intention is the pathway your day will follow, quite like your road map. If you learn to map out your course at the beginning of each new day, you will quickly notice significant differences in your life. For example, in the morning, at the moment you first awake, ponder the possibilities for the new day. What do you really want to do this day? I am not talking about your list of things to do, because we are each very proficient at that practice. I am speaking of what you really, *really* want for your day. How do you want to feel? How do you want to respond to your family and those around you? Think of a person who you want to emulate. Think of your high joy model. Ask yourself what you can do today to be like him or her.

An example of a daily intention might look something like this: "Today I am choosing to be mindful of those around me and to be very courteous in my actions. For today, I will look for the good in all I see and share my findings with others. Today I will act in gratitude for the many gifts I have been given, and I will choose to walk in joy. When I find myself in any other energy I will stop and alter my thoughts."

As you begin writing your intentions, keep them very simple, with only two or three sentences, to ensure your success. Later, when you become more proficient and skilled in this, you can take them to the next level, but in the beginning keep them simple and achievable.

Once you start forming and setting intentions, you will quickly realize how significant this practice is. My first experiences with intentions came from my rapid-eye training. My fellow rapid-eye practitioners and I would have our clients set an intention at the beginning of each session, and then we would add our personal intentions to theirs. I soon realized that their intentions were always met. It is truly an amazing process. This practice of setting intentions then expanded into my personal life. I began setting intentions for specific goals and segments of the day. This is a powerful tool to help you "keep present" and conscious about your life.

Setting daily intentions is a very significant practice, and even though we will not be spending a great deal of time on this process now, I still want to emphasize the importance of setting intentions. Once you begin the process, the fruits will quickly manifest in your life. This is a very simple but powerful process. It is basically stating in a few short sentences what you want for the day or a particular segment of your day. Then as the day moves forward, and perhaps several times throughout the day, simply refocus on your intention, getting into the feeling of the results, and then watch for miracles.

Identifying Your Roadblocks

As we journey through life, we often feel stuck. We feel something is keeping us from where we want to go, but we don't know what it is. In this segment, we are going to take a closer look at what is standing in our way and what we can do about it. We will look at what's blocking us and what is keeping us from accomplishing our goals and establishing the lives of our dreams. We know something is blocking us, but we are blind to what it is.

Our intention now is to discover the answers to the following important questions:
- What is in our way?
- How do we identify what's in the way of our personal goals and desires?
- How do we discover and identify what is keeping us from joy?
- If we identify the roadblocks, what can we do with them?

- How do we remove them?

If while in the process of your day you feel any resistance to setting intentions, or any other process I teach or introduce you to, this is good. This is information. Pay attention to your resistance. Pay attention to your feelings. You can learn a great deal about yourself when you question why you are resisting or experiencing negative feelings. When I have feelings surface that I don't understand, I start asking questions. I want to understand why I feel the way I do.

Here is a great little tool called the "Because Tracks," which will help you discover what is in your way.

The Because Tracks is a digging technique. This process helps to uncover what is underneath our resistance or the cause of our negative feelings. It helps us get to the bottom or the core of the problem. This is our goal.

This technique can be used alone or with a partner, but for our purpose we will discuss how to use it for yourself. In doing so, there are two components working, as if there are two actors on your stage and both of them are you. Each actor will be given a different script. One actor will be the one who is feeling resistance or the negative feeling, and the other actor will be the counselor or therapist, or the one who is going to help you discover why you are resisting. We all have these two parts within.

The first actor begins by stating the negative feeling or belief. The duty of the counselor is to repeat what the first one is feeling and then add the word *because*, which is our digging word. The word *because* works for most situations, but other digging words might be used, such as, "What is under that?" "Go deeper," or "What else is there?" Do you see why I call them digging words? Let's try it out to see how it works.

The words of the first actor, the one who is feeling the negative feelings, are in bold type. The counselor's words will be in italics, and the words of the narrator, me, will be in regular type.

For example, when I feel resistance, I say to myself, **"I am resisting."** Then the counselor in me says, *"I am resisting because?"*

I answer, **"I don't know."**

Then the counselor says, *"You don't know because ... ?"*

Usually at this point, I really don't know, so I think, **"I don't know because ... ?"** And then the answer pops into my head. **"I don't know because ... I don't want to know."**

"You don't want to know, because ... ?"

"I don't want to know because ... ?" Again an answer pops in my head. **"Because then I will have to change."**

"You don't want to change because ... ?"

Pausing, I again think about the question, and then something would come to me.

"Because change is hard, and I am afraid I can't do it."

There. You have just identified what is standing in your way. You have fear standing in your way.

In the beginning, it is easier to do this with a partner than to play both parts, but it can be done.

Once you have identified your roadblock, you have to decide what you want to do with this information. Do you want to be stuck here at this roadblock and not complete your journey, not experience the joy that could be yours? Or do you want to choose again and continue on your way?

When I identify a roadblock, I take it to God and ask Him to help clear and remove my fear, bringing this misconception into resolution and healing. God is waiting on us to ask for His assistance.

Sometimes the element that is keeping me stuck is instantly removed, and sometimes it is not. If it is not instantly removed, I know it is for my greater learning and I then go to the next step.

If it does not go away immediately, I know that the releasing process is as important as having it gone. So I stop there in my journey and begin a new lesson by asking more questions.

In the beginning, while I was learning the process of getting answers to my heartfelt desires—getting answers to my prayers—I would whine quite a bit about not getting my answers immediately. I have learned that when I don't get an answer immediately, it is always for my good. I have discovered that there is something significant I am to learn.

So what if this problem is something you are to learn from? What do you do then?

Well, you simply sit back, open yourself up for the lesson, and watch for it to come. Ask questions. Then trust in Heavenly Father's love. He will always answer your questions in His wisdom and time.

Now sitting back may sound leisurely, but there is more to it than meets the eye. There is action too. The action part is that you are actively engaged in looking for the way heaven is going to respond to you because Heavenly Father always answers the prayer of your heart. Your job is to simply catch them as they come in.

As you participate in each of these processes and become skilled in them, it will feel very familiar, as it should, because being whole and perfect is your true nature.

Note: Simple processes to release your roadblocks will be found in Chapters 16 and 17.

Our Greatest Roadblock to Joy

The greatest roadblock in raising our vibration to a high joy state is the division of our hearts and minds. When your conscious mind wants something and your heart, or your subconscious, wants something else, there is a division. These two parts pull in opposite directions, and here is where you feel and experience struggle. Here is where your battles will always be found. The question is, how do you get these two parts united?

In the beginning of my healing journey, I had no idea how divided I was. The word to describe my personal state of division was *fragmented*. I was divided in so many parts that it was as if I were a giant jigsaw puzzle. I felt helpless and frustrated, and I desperately prayed to God to help make sense of the puzzle of my life. After my prayer, I felt as though God took all the pieces of my life, put them in a bag, shook them up a bit, and then poured them out. Magically, they all began to unite in perfect order. He can do that, you know. He can bring disorder to order and fragmentation into oneness. He can teach us how to help ourselves and how to help others do the same.

Learning where we are divided—where our hearts and minds are pulling against each other—is a significant part of our journey. Discovering our divisions will always involve some kind of subconscious work. It is here that the divisions, separations, and struggles will be uncovered.

The identities given to our two opposing parts are the conscious mind and the subconscious mind. In the spiritual realm, they are called the mind—meaning the conscious mind—and the heart—meaning the core of our being or subconscious mind. When we have perceptions and beliefs written upon our hearts that are not what we really want or are not in line with truth, we experience separation or division. It is actually this part, our subconscious programming, that keeps us in a lower vibrational state, keeps us from the presence of God. The key to living and being in joy is coming into oneness; becoming one heart and one mind; connecting these two opposing parts; and bringing them into resolution, balance, peace, and joy. The fragmentation of these parts will keep you from experiencing the life of your dreams.

Discovering your roadblocks and your divisions will significantly help you on your journey to joy. As you discover each roadblock and clear the way with these wonderful clearing tools and the information in the course, then traveling through life really can become joy filled.

In the beginning of your clearing work, it may feel unfamiliar because it is a new experience. For most people, working in the subconscious realm is something they have never experienced. It feels very much like your dream state. You often wonder if the experience was real and if the memories were real or imagined, which is why working with a practitioner in the beginning is helpful. He or she will validate the memories and what is surfacing for you, giving you the needed boost to continue on your journey. As you trust the experience and yourself and move forward in this, the positive life changes will then be all you need to validate your experience. The results of your participation in this course will make it easy to commit to the work ahead. It is truly wonderful to be clear of old patterns and beliefs. It is great to have your battlefield quiet, to experience peace inside, and to be able to really feel and experience change.

Affirmations

Another great tool that has been around for a time and that will help raise your vibrational offering is affirmations. Have you experienced affirmations?

An affirmation is a short, positive statement affirming who you are or what you want. Many have tried affirmations and have not found the success that others have. Do you know why?

It is because of the division of the heart and mind. When your brain is saying, "I am happy," and you are certainly not feeling that deep in your heart or within your subconscious mind, you will cancel out the affirmation. The key in using affirmations is to keep using them. Do not stop. Our goal is to become happy. We have had "I am not happy" running for a very long time, so until we can get our inside, which is not happy, to be cleared and joyful, we will just be saying words. But is going through the motions or just saying the words important?

Yes.

Why?

When you begin using your positive affirmations and feel a little tug of resistance, or even a big tug, or sometimes feel downright angry at your affirmations, this is good. Why? Because this is important information; you will have just discovered a division. There is something on the inside that is resisting your happiness. Now you know what to do. You know you have some roadwork or clearing to do before you journey on. Every part of this process is important—the positive and the negative. It is all wonderful and helpful; it is just tuning in to why each part is important.

While visiting with an associate in my early rapid-eye training, I was really struck by something he said. "You just triggered me," I informed him as I felt my volcanic emotions starting to rise to the surface. He raised his hand to give me a high five and said, "All right!" At first I was puzzled by his response because I was not feeling very good. To me, this was not a "high five moment." But then I realized, *Yeah, this is good.* I want it to come up and out. So now when I get triggered— whether by affirmation, friend, family member, or life event—it is always good. It is information. The next step is releasing the energy of that emotion or pattern and becoming whole again, reuniting my heart and mind.

Affirmations are a great tool to raise your vibration. You might even consider using this one: "I successfully write and rehearse my affirmations daily."

Tannie Bennett

Writing Personal Affirmations

When you begin to use affirmations, the best ones to use are personal affirmations, the ones you write. Let's write a few together.

Begin by identifying what you want in your life. Some people have a hard time with this one. They have been in the mode of seeing what they don't want for so long that they don't know what they *do* want. So let's start here.

Write what you don't want or don't like in your life. Write things that bug you. Then, when your list is complete, change each item in your list to its opposite, writing what you do like or do want. Change the list a final time to the high vibration form by using the words "I am."

For example, here is something you don't want: "I don't want to be this tired all the time."

You would next write the opposite, which is energetic, vibrant, full of energy. The final step would be to simply write it in the "I am" form: "I am energetic, vibrant, and filled with energy and life."

It is pretty simple.

So we begin by asking ourselves, "What do I really want?"

Most people want love, successful relationships, abundance, and good health, so perhaps that would be a great place to start. We will soon practice writing affirmations, so keep all of your great ideas in mind. Following are a few to get you started, and there are more affirmations at the end of this section and on your CDs.

Affirmation Ideas

- I am growing in health; my body is strong and joyful. I am communicating pleasantly with those I associate with.

- I am gaining wisdom and understanding.
- I am discovering my roadblocks and quickly removing them from my path.
- I am moving forward in joy.
- I am raising my vibration daily, and I am finding joy in this process.
- I am setting daily intentions.
- I express gratitude daily.
- I see the good in everyone, and I give voice to the good I see.
- I am taking care of my wonderful body, and I am filled with light.
- I am filled with love and compassion.
- I am in the flow of abundance.
- I am patient.

In the first run of this course, there was a beautiful young mother in the class. She had three small, busy children, and she was expecting her fourth. One day while discussing the use of the tools, she said, "I simply don't have the time to do all of this, so before I get into the shower each morning, I throw my affirmations over the shower door, and then when I step in and turn the water on, I imagine all of those wonderful affirmations washing over me, filling my life with joy." Everyone loved her idea, and so a new creation was born: "Mimi's Power Shower."

A Quick Review of Simple Techniques to Raise Your Vibrations

- Set daily intentions.
- Identify your roadblocks with prayer or the "Because Tracks."
- Clear the roadblocks with prayer, imagery, the Eight Step Oneness Process or rapid-ye technology, all

of which change your heart or your subconscious programs and beliefs.

- Write and say personal affirmations.
- Take a power shower.

Simple Techniques to Raise Your Vibration

Practice

Write at least ten personal affirmations that are significant and meaningful to you, and say them daily.

Three Steps to Writing Personal Affirmations:

1. Write what you don't want in your life. Example: *"I don't want to be this tired all the time."*
2. Write the opposite of number 1, which is, *"energetic, vibrant, full of energy."*
3. Then write your positive statement in the "I am" form. Example: *"I am energetic, vibrant, and filled with vital energy and life."*

Voila! A personal affirmation has been born.

If you know clearly what you want, you can just write your affirmations without doing steps one and two. However, it is common as we begin our journey to have the majority of our focus on what we don't want.

1._____

_____

_____

2._____

_____

_____

3._____

_____

_____

Tannie Bennett

4._____
_____

5._____
_____

6._____
_____

7._____
_____

8._____
_____

9._____
_____

10._____
_____
_____
_____
_____
_____
_____
_____
_____

A Sample of Daily Affirmations

A special thanks to those who attended my first class and contributed to these affirmations. This is a sample of possibilities. Feel free to create your own; it is a wonderful experience.

I am experiencing another day in paradise. I am guided by my internal guidance system daily. I am a positive, enthusiastic, self-motivated person with a passion for a better lifestyle and the ability to create it. I experience and create music daily. My life is the song of my heart. I am in total harmony with my divine purpose. I am patient. I feel enjoyment throughout my day. I love spending time with my children. I feel love all around me.

I am successful in my business affairs. My family is loving and supportive. I accomplish great things. I am assisting my children in recognizing and developing their talents. I am a loving and supportive companion. I am healthy. I am loved. Money flows fluidly into my life. I am financially wise. I am spiritual. I am a glorious child of God, and He loves me. I am supported by the powers of heaven. I am lovable and capable.

I am a high joy vibration that vibrates joy and vibrant life to those around me. I am whole and healed, and I feel magnificent. I am beautiful. I am thankful for all my blessings and vocalize them daily. I am thankful for my Savior. I am grateful for my angels who help me with my creations. I am open to receive the abundance that is there for me. I am trusting. I am healthy and vibrant. I am responsible. I am joyous. I am supported and loved. I am deserving.

I am happy. I accept myself, my spouse, my family, my children, and my relatives as they are. I love everyone, and everyone loves me. I sparkle wherever I am. I am healthy, and my body naturally desires wholesome, live foods. I am beautiful and graceful. The law of the Lord is abundance; I gratefully accept all the abundance that flows to me, and I act in gratitude for it. I am grateful for the angelic assistance given to me to orchestrate the details of my life. I experience all my relationships as glorious, rewarding, and fulfilling. I am thoughtful and patient.

I allow others to create their own experience without judgment. I work quickly and effortlessly each day with divine assistance to organize and simplify my life so that order, cleanliness, and peace may abide. My home is a high vibration where the light of Christ perfectly dwells. I am forgiving and unconditionally loving. I am grateful for the abundance of good in all areas of my life. I am letting go and allowing myself and others to reach our highest potential.

I am beautiful, joyful, happy, and smiling. I am loved. I am worthwhile. I am thankful for the experiences that bring me understanding and growth. I am thankful for the abundance of cash and wealth that flows into my life so easily. My prayers are answered, and I can clearly understand these answers. I am grateful. I am thankful for my healthy body that works properly and perfectly. I live an intentional, joy-filled life.

I am grateful for the feelings of peace and joy that abound in me. I see the good in all of the events and details of my life. I create more and more experiences that generate feelings of joy in my life. I am experiencing my body as balanced and filled with vital energy. My sleep is magnified, and I wake up each day refreshed and joyful to begin the new day. I am clear about what I want to create in my life, and I set clear daily intentions. I am grateful to be alive and for the experiences my wonderful body is giving me.

All parts of me are awakening to my truth. I am accepting and allowing my journey and my lessons to take whatever time is needed. I am finding joy in the journey and process. I am doing what I want each day and giving myself plenty of playtime to do it. I am balanced in work and play. I am aware that the body is the vehicle to learn all the experiences and lessons I signed up for. I offer love and gratitude to my body each day for its service to me.

I view my opposition as a gifted teacher. I know that unconditional love befalls as I become grateful for my opposition. I do all things with intention. All my needs and desires are met. I am free of the burden and power money has over me. I am free of past illusions and mistakes. I am generous with my abundance. I celebrate my and others' success daily. I surround myself with things that reflect vitality and joy. I am achieving my dreams. I am doing what I love. I am love.

I am healthy and strong and enjoying my life. I am building a glorious mansion with my thoughts. I am enough, I am complete, and I am an important part of God's work. I am following a great path and am moving forward in it daily. I am loved and have many wonderful new friends. I am a healer; I am helping others move forward. I have an abundance of all that my family needs. I am living in a state of joy and gratitude for the journey that I am on. I am comfortable in my own skin and love being me!

I enjoy my special gifts. I am grateful for the discoveries I am making about my gifts, and I am excited to use them to help Heavenly Father in His work and to bless the lives of my fellow men. There is abundance in my life, which I freely give to others. I am energetic. I feel vibrant, alive, and energized all day long. I am important, needed, and loved. I feel the love of others; I feel the love Heavenly Father generously offers. I hear answers to my questions clearly, and I understand what steps to take next. I see my life unfolding before me, and I am willing, ready, and able to follow the path.

I am in tune with God's will. I am one with God, and I am in harmony with divine law. I have the energy of a two-year-old! I gratefully accept the abundance Heavenly Father sends. I am growing from grace to grace, becoming the gracious person I am meant to be. I am willing to let God carry my burdens. I am an instrument of light and hope. I consistently reflect God's love and light to others.

9

Raising Your Vibration through Breath Work and Imagery

The Gift of Deep Breathing

The following techniques are very simple in nature, so please do not discount their effectiveness or importance because of their simplicity. They are very powerful techniques, but they will help only if you use them.

The first technique I would like to introduce is basic, deep belly breathing. Breathing is something you do every day. It is estimated that we will take more than 500 million breaths in our lifetime. Something we do that much has got to be important. We all know the simple significance of breathing; if we don't breathe we don't live. But there is so much more to breathing than just getting by and staying alive.

Let's first learn the belly breathing technique.

Begin by placing your hands on your waist, with your index fingers positioned just under the last rib and your thumbs in back. Now squeeze your thumb and fingers together in the general area of your waist, as if you're squishing a small balloon. Now breathe in deeply, filling your lower lungs. As you do so, your enlarged diaphragm will push your fingers and thumbs apart, as if enlarging the balloon by blowing into it. As the air flows deep into the lower lungs, filling your lungs to capacity, your fingers will naturally be pushed apart from your thumbs.

Try this deep belly breathing technique a few times. When you exhale, bring your fingers and thumbs together. When you inhale, your fingers should still be tight on your waist, or that general area, but your breath will be the force that pushes them apart.

Please take a moment now to breathe deeply ten to twenty times.

How do you feel? Do you detect any difference in the way you feel?

If you are unable to detect a difference now, it is okay. You will as soon you make deep belly breathing a significant part of your day.

Let's take a minute to go over a few of the benefits of this process. Begin by thinking about your life for a moment. Just take a quick scan of it, and then reflect on the following statement: *When you cease to breathe, you cease to live.*

How are you doing? Would you say in reference to your life that you are really living?

What does it mean to you to "really live"?

You have likely heard someone say, "They are really living a full life." What do you imagine a full life would be like?

Are you living a full life?

Most of us are barely getting by. Did you know that your lifestyle is directly connected to your breathing? I have discovered that people who are depressed, anxiety ridden, stress filled, mentally ill, and even those experiencing heart failure are barely breathing. They breathe from the upper chest, where there is little blood exchange, and therefore they are barely alive. Those who have embarked on focused breathing as a daily routine literally come alive. Their lives start to significantly improve as they focus on breath work and practice this simple technique ten to twenty minutes a day.

Did you know that if you breathe properly, you will not be able to go into fear or stress? That's right; you cannot be in stress or fear if you are breathing regular, slow, focused, diaphragmatic breaths. Diaphragmatic breathing will also significantly reduce the pain you feel. Pain is a message that there is need for a shift, a change in what you're doing. For instance, if you were to put your hand on a hot stove, you would feel pain; the message is to remove your hand from the heat. Our bodies are always sending us messages. Do we attune ourselves to the simple messages of pain? I know I certainly have been guilty of ignoring them. This is another area that will improve as you attune yourself to it and regularly practice deep, diaphragmatic breathing.

We can't change anything without first attuning ourselves to the need for the change. For example, if you pay attention to your breathing, you will notice that when you are stressed or in significant pain, you are not breathing properly. Anxiety is strong emotion without breath. This could also be said of most negative emotions and pain; they come in without the breath. Pay attention to this. When you are feeling strong pain, notice your breathing. I have often caught myself holding my breath when in severe pain.

Years ago while praying for help, the Spirit told me I needed more oxygen. I pondered this and thought, *Well, I breathe every day. How else do I get more oxygen?* I didn't get it at first, but as time passed I began to understand the Spirit's instruction. Once I finally understood what I was to do, my life took a great leap forward. I began to experience the benefits of deep breathing, and I loved it. I posted little "Breathe" signs all over my house and in my car to remind me to breathe deeply. Now it's automatic. I deep breathe with my clients at the beginning of each session. I deep breathe when I feel negative emotion surface. I deep breathe when I begin my meditations and prayers, when I begin to deeply concentrate, before I go to sleep every night and the first thing when I awake. This has now become a habit and a very significant part of my life. When I began my deep breathing practice, I was using an oxygen-condensing machine every night. If I failed to use it or if my nasal tube fell off during the night, I would wake up with a splitting headache. I would then simply put my oxygen tube back on and take a few deep breaths, and my headache would quickly go away.

One evening as I prepared for bed and put my oxygen tube on, I heard the Spirit whisper, "You don't need that anymore." I dropped the tube to the floor and got in bed. For the first time in years, I slept without oxygen. It was a joy to have healed that part of my life. In the past, I had to carry this large oxygen-condensing machine with me wherever I traveled. I affectionately named it O2D2. Now I am free. I can sleep without needing to have O2D2 purring at my side. I can now go camping with my kids.

Deep breathing has become a very significant part of my life. One Sunday while attending church, I caught myself starting to breathe deeply as I closed my eyes to pray. I had to chuckle at the new neuropathway I had formed, which was, "When I close my eyes, I start to deep breathe." It is now automatic, and I love it.

I have noticed that when my clients, or anyone really, are under severe stress, their breathing is very shallow. I think the most significant example of this was of a client who was brought in to see me the day after her suicide attempt. When I started the session with deep breathing, I was stunned to see that she could not even take a deep breath. She looked asthmatic, which she was not. She could barely get the breath past her throat. Breath is life. When we don't want to be here any longer, we stop breathing. If you want to change your life, breathe!

Intentional breath work is a simple process we can do anywhere and at anytime. When I am at home and stressed for any reason, if my children are nearby and conscious of my state, they will often get right in my face and say, "Mom, breathe." Then they'll work with me, coaching me until I have shifted out of my stress mode. I love them for that. I don't even remember teaching them to do it, but I am very grateful that they do.

If you want to have a more joyful life,
begin by adding life to your joy. Breathe.

Start taking life in fully and letting go of things that don't serve you, as you do with breath work. We inhale the future and exhale the past. We breathe in fresh oxygen; we breathe out carbon dioxide, a waste product. Take into your life what you want and breathe out what you don't want. It is pretty simple.

Think of childbirth. Would you consider any part of that process stressful or painful? Now consider how women are often coached in breath work to get through childbirth.

When you begin to become conscious of your breathing,
you will become conscious of your life.

We need a breathing coach to help us through Life

Not Just Birth

The Benefit of Imageries—Creating Your Blueprint for Change

Typically, guided imageries are used in a therapeutic environment because of the wealth of benefits they offer to the human mind and soul. The first and most significant purpose in using imageries is to relax the body. We are living in a fast-paced world; we struggle to receive the rest and recuperation time we need to keep our bodies in perfect running condition. Participating in imageries will allow the body time to experience deep relaxed states. Choosing this as part of your daily routine will be the equivalent of receiving an extra three to four hours of good sleep for a simple thirty- to forty-minute imagery.

During the imaging process, the brain will float back and forth between the varying brain wave states, the same states that occur during your sleep. As your body goes in and out of these states, a significant amount of healing will occur because your sleeping period is your body's natural healing time. This is why rest and sleep are so vital when you are sick. It is during this sleep period that the body is doing its major repairs. If you go for an extended period of time without sleep, your body and mind quickly fall into disrepair and pain. Sleep is so significant that if you are deprived of it for a lengthy period of time, your body begins to die. Sleep is as essential to your health as breath itself, although the body can survive longer without sleep than it can without breath. Nonetheless, it is important to understand just how vital your sleep is.

Experiencing focused meditation and focused imageries on a daily basis will significantly improve your state of health and well-being. Most often we receive this type of healing in a counselor's, psychotherapist's, or hypnotist's office. In this environment, the benefits are limited because of the intent of the visit. Usually, we are there on a crisis-to-crisis basis; thus, we are unable to fully relax and receive the complete benefit of the process.

Having an opportunity to experience guided imageries in your own home is significant. You will experience these imageries during a time that is most significant to you, and you will be in an environment that is tailored to your comfort and security. This comfortable environment will greatly enhance the benefits of participating in guided imageries because you choose the time. It is an activity you participate in because you understand the extensive benefits of the process. It is something you desire to do, thus altering the experience in a grand way from the previously mentioned scenario. Anytime we bring a life situation to a point of choice and proceed with that intention, the benefits are greatly enhanced because we feel free, a law that God himself perfectly honors. Our freedom is essential to our happiness, and having the power to choose is very significant in any moment in life. As you choose this type of healing, you will begin an amazing journey.

There are other benefits in doing guided imageries in the privacy of your home and in the time and place you choose. One is that you give a message to your body that you are important. When you take time out to take care of yourself by doing things that are for your good, your body responds in a very significant way. It will respond with health.

Our bodies are designed to respond quickly to the compliance of natural laws. For example, if we were unaware of the law of gravity and stepped out of a two-story window, our body would respond with a message of pain, informing us that a natural law was unheeded. When we respect natural laws and are educated in them, our bodies respond with health. If we are ignorant of them, nature will still take its toll, causing us pain and discomfort.

Your body is made up of intelligences, tiny little entities that go about honoring the roles God gave to them. This is why our bodies work in such an amazing fashion without our having to direct each and every process. Having to think about everything the body does in and of itself would be too cumbersome for the human mind, and little growth would take place. Can you imagine having to think about digesting your food, about pumping your blood, or taking air in and pushing it out of your lungs? It would be absolutely overwhelming to think of all that you would need to keep your body moving from moment to moment. This is why God designed our bodies to be self-cleaning, self-propelling, self-healing, magnificent machines.

Even though our bodies are truly amazing machines made up of intelligent matter, we still have a significant role in managing them. It is our role and responsibility to learn the natural laws that govern these miraculous bodies that God gave us. One significant law that we would do well to understand is the role of rest. Rest is essential to the health and well-being of your body. Each day, you are given the choice of whether or not you are going to honor this law. If you choose to honor it, you will receive the blessings from that choice; if you choose to ignore it, you will receive the consequences of that choice. Each moment of our lives, we have the right to choose, and each moment we reap the benefits or consequences of those choices.

Because we are living in such a fast-paced society, it is important to help our bodies meet the demands that are placed upon them. We spend more time putting out and less time resting up than we should; therefore, we are putting undue demands upon our physical bodies and reaping the consequences of those choices. Visualization is a simple process and a treasure of knowledge that will assist you in caring for your precious body.

Many benefits can be derived from spending time in the imagery process. By nature, we are creators like our Father in Heaven. During our imagery time, we can draw up the blueprint of our day's creation. Failing to create a blueprint of a house we want to build could have disastrous results. Yet each day we go about our lives without ever spending time in the drawing room, engaging in our creative process. We just start the day with the attitude of "another day …," and indeed that is what we get: "another day."

If we want something more out of life than we are presently receiving, then we must take time out to create it by drawing up the perfect blueprint of our hearts' desires.

Remember in your youth how you had such dreams and hopes? Now, in looking back at our lives, we wonder how we got to where we are today, perhaps thinking, *Boy, life sure didn't turn out like I wanted it to.* "Why?" you might ask. Our lives didn't turn out because we stopped focusing on our dreams and started focusing on what we didn't want. Now is the time to dream and create again.

Remember the law of the harvest or the law of attraction: you reap what you sow. If you do not spend time each and every day drawing up the blueprint of your life and your day, you will reap the results of your failure to consciously create. You will create whatever you put your focus on or whatever has been prerecorded. It's easy to focus on our trials and pains, and so we continue to create more of what we don't want. Now it's time to create what you do want.

Using imagery to create is a wonderful process. When you are relaxed and your brain is pulsating in the alpha brainwave state, you are able to absorb more information than you normally would. When you create in this relaxed state, your brain receives this information on a much deeper level; as a result, you will spend less time in "doing" and more time in "being." Your whole system will work with you to accomplish your goal, rather than having the normal 10 percent working for you and the other 90 percent working against you. You will give your whole being the message that this is the desired goal.

When you send your brain messages in pictures (images), it is the equivalent of having your blueprint developed on all levels. All of the little intelligences in your body get the picture of the desired goal. They will all be working for you rather than against you. It is like you are laying down the program for your brain computer to run on. It will know what to do after it is successfully programmed. You too will know what to do after you program through imagery. An old saying applies here: "If you fail to plan, you plan to fail." Become an intentional creator of your life; use imagery daily.

Focused Imagery or Intentional Visualization Summary and Review

Imagery work is a simple process that uses your mind and imagination. Using imageries can have a profound effect on your life. Everyone can imagine; therefore, everyone can be successful with this process. This is something you can do by yourself once you learn how. You will be given many opportunities to practice imagery throughout this course. As you faithfully participate in the recorded imageries, you will begin to experience the gift this process can be to your life. (The recorded Journey to Joy imageries may be found in the audio version of this book, or sold separately.)

The Imagery Process

- First, relax your body by getting comfortable, and begin your focused deep breathing. Once you feel relaxed and have fully oxygenated your body, choose your intention.
- State your intention out loud or in your mind. Adding intention to your imagery session is very important. Each imagery in this course has a specific intention. Some imageries are intended to simply release negative emotion, some are to help you create and clarify what you want, and some are to help you recreate a memory that will facilitate your joy-filled journey. Even though you may use the same imagery over and over again, every imagery session experience will be different because your personal intentions will change the outcome. *It is important to remember to add your personal intention to the imagery before the session begins.*
- Experience the imagery. It is helpful to close your eyes during the imagery session to help you focus

your mind on your intentions and provide an environment that will help you to connect to the mental images, the feelings, and the spirit within. Once the imagery is complete, you will begin the emergence process.

- Emerging is the process of coming back into your fully awakened state. After your imagery session is complete, deep breathe again and open your eyes. Allow yourself some good wake-up time. (The emergence process is taught in Chapter 24, *How to Use Journey to Joy Imageries.*)

The Significance of Metaphors in the Imagery Process

In the *Webster's New World Dictionary 4th edition*, *metaphor* is defined as a figure of speech in which one thing is likened to another.

Christ, while living upon the earth, used metaphors to teach things of heaven to those he ministered to. He used what the people of his time were familiar with. This enabled him to bring what they had forgotten back into their remembrance. Throughout the scriptures, the prophets and writers of the holy word used metaphors. Additionally, those who interpreted dreams, like Joseph, interpreted the metaphors.

You use metaphors every day of your life. In the scriptures, we read, "Another parable put he forth unto them, saying, The kingdom of heaven is likened unto a man which sowed good seed in his field" (Matt. 13:24 KJV).

The use of metaphors in teaching and in imagery is intended to help produce a clearer picture of what you want. When you compare your life to "a stage," it instantly conjures up a picture, and more is taught with the picture than the few words you choose. It is like getting a double lesson. It is also easier to remember pictures and stories than instruction. Using metaphors in our imageries and sessions helps us remember because the metaphors are images we can relate to.

When in session with clients, it is a very natural thing to use metaphors. They help in many ways. When you are connecting to a huge fear, for instance, it is a lot easier to see it in a symbol than to again experience the total memory. You can face for instance a big rock a lot easier than the details of a huge trauma. This also works for the positive elements of our sessions. When clients visualize in their minds a being of light taking them into a huge cavern of unlimited treasures which represents their gifts from God, they get a very clear picture of the magnitude of God's love for them and who they really are.

Imagery work and the use of metaphors is the work of the divine. It is the language of the spirit. You will love your imagery experiences once you walk through this door.

What Can We Gain by Using Imageries, and Why Are They Important?

Focused meditation and intentional imageries are ways to give your body a message of love. They can provide a time to fully oxygenate your body. As you go into the deeper relaxed states of consciousness, a significant amount of healing will occur because your sleeping period is your body's natural healing time. When you take time out to participate in a twenty- to thirty-minute imagery, it is the equivalent of receiving three to four hours of sound sleep, sleep that perhaps you normally would not get.

When you are in a relaxed state and using imagery, your whole being gets the picture of what you want. This is very powerful. This is one reason television is so influential. We are relaxed when we watch it, and it is able to go in to deeper levels of our minds.

Knowing this fact, my son once said to me, "Mom, why don't they put math class on a video so I can get it on a deeper level?"

When you relax your body with intention, deep breathe with intention, and image with intention, you are creating a powerful healing tool.

The power will, however, depend upon your intentions, what you are there to accomplish. My intention is to be in joy and to heal my life; therefore, every imagery in this course is intended to help in a step-by-step process attain that goal.

Think for a moment—what do you want in your life? Make a list of your ideas; write them in your workbooks.

If you were to spend a few minutes each day getting a very clear picture of what you want and reviewing it in your imagery meditation time, you would be amazed at the results.

This is how all the great men and women of the world achieved their goals. They imagined themselves attaining their goals before it happened. How big can you dream?

Raising Your Vibration through Breath Work and Imagery Meditation

Practice

What do you want in your life? Create a very clear picture. This can be a running list; you may add to it as new possibilities come into your mind. Review this daily in your imagery meditation time. You will be amazed at the results.

_____
_____
_____
_____
_____
_____
_____
_____
_____
_____
_____
_____
_____
_____
_____
_____
_____
_____
_____
_____
_____
_____
_____
_____

10
Love: The Power That Heals

Love itself is the healing power. If you want to heal your life, begin with love.

There have been many books written about the healing power of love, but it wasn't until I was in the process of writing my own book that I began to understand this divine principle.

Working as an energy practitioner, I have had the opportunity of meeting many wonderful individuals who are dedicated to healing. One particular family, who experienced the miraculous healing power of love, stands out in my mind.

This family was going through some very difficult trials. The father had AIDS and was physically very ill. As I watched his family go through this experience, I was profoundly impressed with the integrity and strength of his wife. I will always esteem her as a true follower of Christ.

I talked to her after she discovered her husband's condition and his choices that led to it. Her virtue and faith were inspiring. She had a steely determination to stand by his side. She loved him and knew even in this circumstance that he was a great man.

In the beginning, because of his fear and his illness, he was unable to see the gift of love she offered. But soon the fruits of forgiveness and love began to quickly manifest in their lives. I was blessed to witness their miracle. I was blessed to witness the power of her gift of unconditional love. It was a beautiful life story to behold.

I watched the gentleman regain his health to the point that there was no apparent evidence of the disease in his body. She never contracted the disease. His life healed, their marriage healed, and their family healed. I know it was a difficult experience to go through, but from this experience grew the gift of a miracle. I became a witness to "the healing power of love."

I have witnessed similar scenarios in other families that did not generate the same results simply because unconditional love was not present in the experience. The wife and the husband were fearful and unforgiving. The results created more opposition in their lives and in the lives of the children.

The first place we learn about love is in our homes. For many, the learning is insufficient because of the abuse and dysfunction that took place within the home environment. Some of you are blessed to have had wonderful parent models. Regardless of individual scenarios, today we are going to start from the beginning. We are going to assume that you know nothing about love.

In the beginning of your life, you were born into opposition; you were born into the opposite of your heavenly home, which is the opposite of love. You are here to gain experience in opposition—to learn, grow, and make choices and eventually return to your heavenly home filled with love.

So if we are here experiencing the opposite of love, what would you call this experience? What is the opposite of love?

The opposite of love is anything unlike pure, unconditional love. This whole experience is filled with the opposite of love. We give the opposite of love many names, but it is this very experience we are going through. Ranae Johnson, founder of the Rapid Eye Institute, has often said, "There are only two emotions: love and love misused." That makes it pretty simple, doesn't it?

Love is the power that creates. Love is the power that moves the stars in the heavens. Love is the power that called us into being. Love is the power of God. It is because of love that He exists. "God is love; and he that dwelleth in love dwelleth in God and God in him" (1 John 4:16 KVJ).

I believe that the very plan and purpose of life came into existence because of God's love. We are here because of this love. We are saved because of His love for us, and we have all that we have because of God's love for us.

Everything is because of love.

Now, if this is true, then don't you think love is important to have in your life? Shouldn't love be in and throughout all of your life? Love should fill the immensity of your space. Love was meant to be felt in every aspect of your life.

So what is the problem?

Why are we not feeling and experiencing the love of God?

What is getting in the way of having this experience on a moment-to-moment basis?

What is blocking our feelings? If love is in and through all things, why are we not feeling it?

Did you know that you *are* feeling it? Each and every day, you feel the love of God, but you do not recognize it as His love. To you, it feels more like pain, sorrow, sadness, anger, and deep grief or all the other feelings you have felt.

"What?" you may ask. "Are you saying the negative feelings we feel are also a part of God's love?"

Yes, that is exactly what I am saying.

You see, God loved you so much that He provided a plan in which you could learn and grow to be like Him. It is called the Great Plan of Happiness. This plan provided us an opportunity to come to earth and receive bodies. While we are here we learn, grow, and progress to eventually become like our Father in Heaven, we have an opportunity to experience opposition and experience our magnificence. And guess what? You are experiencing this day to day. You are here learning to make choices moment by moment. You are learning from these choices what you want to experience and what you don't want to experience. You are learning from this experience the cause-and-effect principle: if I make this choice, I will get these results. You are learning from these choices how to call upon God for your daily assistance, and you are learning how strong you are—look at what you have championed already. You are making it!

Are you ready to find love in every part of your day?

Are you ready to see the love of God in every facet of your life? He is there!

> "Earth is filled with Heaven.
> Every common bush a flame with God,
> But only he who sees takes off his shoes."
> —Author unknown

We came into this physical realm so that we might comprehend all things and so that the eyes of our understanding might be opened. We are here to learn and grow. We are here to experience opposition so that we can follow in God's footsteps and walk as one with Him.

You are right on course! You are doing the very thing you came here to do.

So instead of thinking you are doing something wrong, realize that you are doing something right. Your opposition is intended to bring you closer to God because He too experienced opposition. He experienced the full course of opposition, and for our lifetime we experience only a measure of it. We are experiencing the courses we chose to experience in our beginning.

Our concluding message is this: there are other ways to learn. When the student is ready, the teacher appears. You can experience opposition in joy or in sorrow. It is all a matter of choice. We can choose to battle, or we can choose to feel the love of God.

It is time to start your course—your schooling—feeling the love of God in every part of your day. It is time to look at your opposition in a different way. It is time to be kind and loving to yourself. It is time to feel and know how wonderful you are and to see your magnificence. It is time to know that you are really doing a great job and realize that you are doing what you came to do. No one can live your life any better than you can. You are perfect, you are experiencing all the tough trials you signed up for, and now you're ready to learn a different way. You are ready to experience opposition in joy.

How do you experience opposition in joy? Simply by looking for it; it is there. Remember that God is in and through all things. Look for Him in every aspect of your day. Try to find His presence in your greatest trial.

"And God saw every thing that he had made, and, behold, it was very good" (Gen. 1:31 KJV).

Look for the good in every particle of your life; both positive and negative elements are there. What are you going to focus on? You have spent a great deal of time in trials and pain because of your early perceptions and programming. This is what your focus has been on. Now it is time to change the experience and focus on the good.

Is it possible to change your focus midexperience? Is it possible to look for the good while in stress–filled, negative situations?

I believe it is. Allow me to share a personal experience.

Finding the Gift of Love in Opposition

Early one morning as I was preparing to leave for an advanced training in Oregon at the Rapid Eye Institute, I decided to pray for guidance and assistance. While in the midst of my prayer, I asked God if there were any particular instructions for this trip. I was simply told to "be in the flow." This seemed an unusual instruction. Not totally understanding the message, I simply trusted and filed it in my mind, and I headed for Oregon.

The first day of the training, everyone met together for a "get acquainted" dinner. I looked around for old friends, and I found an acquaintance from Utah who had traveled to Oregon on his motorcycle. During the course of our conversation, we discussed going for a ride together. This was a step out of my box. I had been in a shell for so very long.

The last day of the training arrived, and I thought, in reference to the motorcycle ride, "Whatever happens is perfect," not knowing if he remembered our conversation. By that time, I had already had a great time just thinking about it.

During our last lunch at the institute, he slipped up behind me and said, "If you want to ride, you'd better hurry. I'll meet you out front." I quickly finished and met him outside. As we put our helmets on, he instructed me in the basics of leaning into the turns. I had ridden a motorcycle before, but it had been a very long time.

I got on the back of his bike, and we were off! He took the first couple of turns slowly. I was able to catch my breath and lean properly, although I wanted to lean the other way—against the turn, in the opposite direction.

It was quite an experience. I held on tight as we zipped down the road. I delighted in the fragrance of the great outdoors and the smell of his leather jacket as it pierced my nose. It was great!

Then the road quickly changed. It became very curvy. He no sooner took one curve than it was time to take the next. I no longer had the luxury of a five-minute recovery time between curves. It was one right after the other. My stomach tightened along with my grip. I became fearful. At this time, the Spirit's instructions to "be in the flow" came into my mind. I pondered this.

Here we were, two people on the same bike having the same ride, but we were definitely not having the same experience. I thought, *Well, Tannie, Lenard loves this. Now you can be in the flow with this and have his experience, or you can be in fear and uptight and have your experience. What experience do you want? Do you want to have a great time, or do you want to be in fear?*

I decided I had been in fear long enough. I was going to let go and flow with this. I was going to change my focus to one of joy, like Lenard's. I then let go of my death grip. As soon as I let go, Lenard's hands came up underneath mine, raising my hands and arms with his parallel to the ground, as if we were flying. No one was driving the bike. I closed my eyes as tears of joy slipped down my face. I had let go of fear. I had changed my focus. I was in the flow, and we were soaring. I chose joy.

We can change midexperience. We can make each experience a love- and joy-filled one, or we can be in a negative energy. It is our choice.

How do you choose love and joy? How do you make it your focus?

- By looking at all that you love in your life
- By looking at all that you love about yourself
- By looking at all that you love about your family
- By looking at all that you love about your job
- By looking at all that you love about your financial situation
- By looking at all that you love about your greatest trial

But the most profound change will occur in your life when you not only look at the good or the positive but feel it in the depth of your heart. When you can feel how awesome you are and how wonderful all the different aspects of your life are, then you will begin a mighty change.

Love:
The Power That Heals

Practice

In every life situation, there is a gift of love hidden in the framework of the experience. When we experience a life situation from the point of view of "Man, this really stinks," then that opening statement actually frames our experience. It then becomes a negative situation. If we have the wisdom to look at a life situation from the highest point of view—perhaps "This is for my good, or there is something great to learn from this experience"—then that will be the framework of our experience. Each experience provides a gift. Do we have the wisdom to look for the gift in the beginning of the experience?

Below are questions that will help you get into the mindset of positive framing. Once you answer the questions, you will basically have the raw material to build the framework of a great life. You will have the framework to experience your opposition in joy.

Choosing Love and Joy as Your Focus: Creating a Positive Frame

1. Look at everything you love about your life and record your findings. Review this list often.
2. Make a list of everything that you love about yourself, your family, your job, and your financial situation. Then complete your lists with anything else that seems to be significant to you and your life situation.

3. Make a list of everything you have learned about your greatest trial and why it is a gift to your experience.

Once you have a list of all that you love about your life, you will begin to experience a mighty change of heart. When you begin to see each of your life experiences from a love-and-joy point of view, you will begin to experience joy as you have never felt it before. Once this list is well developed, it will be easy to quickly move into gratitude for the experiences you once framed negatively. Even in the most trying of circumstances, you will be able to quickly shift your emotions into a positive framework and then those around you will marvel at your strength and attitude. But the greatest gift from this experience will be the joy you constantly harbor in your heart.

_____

_____

_____

_____

_____

_____

_____

_____

_____

_____

_____

_____

_____

_____

_____

_____

_____

_____

_____

_____

11

True Service

How do you help others?

By holding an image of their perfection always in your mind.

Tannie Bennett

Frequently we see loved ones in their trials and in opposition, and our hearts naturally reach out to help them. I have spent many years not knowing how to significantly help my friends and loved ones in their trials, until recently when I asked that very question.

Late one evening, I was driving my daughter along her newspaper route. The day had been very busy, and we didn't get to delivering the papers until after ten o'clock that evening. As we were driving the route, we drove by a friend's house. The lights were out, but I could dimly see my friend pacing back and forth in her driveway. We threw her the paper, and then I heard her call to me. I stopped the car, and she came over and said, "Tannie, you won't have to deliver papers here anymore." I could tell by the sound of her voice that she had been crying. I asked her if I could do anything for her. She said, "Well ..." and then proceeded to tell me a bit more about her situation. She said, "I'll be okay. Thanks, anyway." And then she went inside.

I began to pray for her. I very specifically asked Heavenly Father how I could help or serve her best. He told me to ask to see her spiritual contracts. Surprised at this, I asked, "Can I see her spiritual contracts?" When they were opened up to me, I saw what she wanted to become. She wanted to become a strong woman of great faith, like Queen Esther in the Bible. *Wow*, I thought. Then the Spirit asked me, "How is she doing on that goal?" I quickly reviewed her trials; they were many and great! Then I understood the lesson. She was well on her way to becoming a woman of great strength and faith like Queen Esther.

Still feeling compassion for her situation, I asked, "Is there anything I can do to help her?" The Spirit responded, "You can pray for her as the angels do to be strengthened in her trials, and you can love her." I did as the Spirit directed me, and I was again taught a valuable lesson. Our trials—our opposition—are the very tools that help us become the masterpiece we want to become. Like a jewel being polished by abrasive sand, our opposition helps to knock off our rough outer edges, and soon our masterpiece, our Queen Esther, begins to emerge.

We each have a desire to serve our fellow man, yet it is important to know that true service is never a burden. It is always a joy. When I have a desire to serve a specific individual, I always begin with prayer. Everyone is unique and has specific needs.

Here is an example of my simple prayer of service, offered on another's behalf.

Heavenly Father,
It is my intention to serve (name). Please help and inspire me on their behalf.

I then wait for an idea or some inspired thought to present itself in my mind. If nothing comes quickly to my mind, I continue to pray.

Heavenly Father, would you please help (name) in their trials. Bless them to get the greater learning this situation is trying to teach them and strengthen them to be able to endure the experience until they get the learning they intended on in their beginnings. If this is a pattern that they are ready to heal from, please heal it and restore them to their original blueprint.
Thank you, Heavenly Father,
In the name of Jesus Christ. Amen.

The significance of this type of service is that you are not taking any liberty with that person's life. You are leaving it all in God's hands. You simply offered a prayer of support. If inspired thought comes, it will usually be in response to something the person is asking God for. By opening yourself up to serve and support, God can then use you as His emissary to serve that individual in a way that honors his or her growth and use of agency.

If service feels burdensome to you, you are out of alignment with either your desires and needs or those of the person you're serving. If you are in need of further enlightenment with regard to serving your fellow man, ask God for direction and inspiration. He will support you in the desires of your heart, and you will gain great understanding and knowledge as you ask for direction. He can reveal to you what is in the way of service or what is out of alignment.

Remember that true service always brings joy to both the giver and the receiver.

Years ago, when my children were very young, I met a wonderful woman of great faith. She was a storyteller by nature and would often share her personal experiences with me. I enjoyed visiting with her and hearing the stories she told. One particular story stands out in my mind.

My friend Donna had a huge heart. She loved and served everyone around her, even the critters that fell from the sky. She was Dr. Mom for the entire neighborhood.

She had six children naturally, adopted five, and was a foster mother to who knows how many children. Suffice it to say that she had a lot of love for everyone.

Even though she had an abundance of love, money was in short supply around her house. Yet she managed.

Donna had a passion for service. She decided one day that she was going to adopt four foreign siblings in the hopes of giving them a better life. To do so, she and her husband sold almost everything they had to pay for their passage and the adoption expenses. When the children arrived, they had many needs. The family stretched the budget as much as they could, but it wasn't enough. One of the unmet needs was bath towels. Having such a large family, they went through towels very quickly. There never seemed to be enough.

Donna did what she always did—she turned to God for help. She prayed for towels.

Soon there came a knock at her door. On the other side was a woman, an acquaintance of theirs who lived down the street. She looked at Donna with a puzzled expression and said, "I know this is going to sound strange, but Donna, could you use some bath towels?"

Donna was stunned. "Yes," she said. "I need them very badly."

"Well, here then." The woman then turned around, picked up a huge stack of bath towels, and handed them to Donna.

"How did you know?" Donna asked, as tears of gratitude welled up in her eyes.

"Well, as I was praying this morning, the Spirit told me to take you a large stack of bath towels. I felt a little strange doing this, but I have always tried to trust the promptings of my heart. I am glad you needed them. I had plenty, and I am happy to share."

Donna gave her benefactor a huge hug, thanked her profusely, and went inside to thank Heavenly Father for hearing and answering the prayer of her heart.

True service is always a joy; it's two hearts becoming one. One has a need to receive, and one has a desire to give. Then God magically brings the two together, and you get one big miracle and a lot of happy people.

Everyone is on target for the life they choose to experience and the lessons they choose to learn. Our job is to trust that.

12
Spiritual Contracts

A long time ago, before you were born—when you were in the sprit realm with your heavenly family—you watched the creation of the earth unfold. After the earth was created and you knew of the plan to people the earth, which included the opportunity to obtain a physical body, you knew you wanted to be a part of that plan. You knew you wanted to gain a physical body and experience life in that wonderful place.

The earth was so beautiful. To think you had the opportunity to be involved in such a great experience caused unimaginable joy. Once it became known that you would indeed have the opportunity to experience the earth and life on it, you then began to choose the experiences you wanted to have. At that time, you were informed by your heavenly parents of the era in which you would experience life on earth. You were told of the events that would take place on the earth during your generation. There would be many great and important events, and you were excited to have the opportunity to come at that time because of these events.

During your generation, there would be a lot of confusion on the earth. There would be many strong and influential voices pulling you in every direction. This concerned you, but when you had the opportunity to spend time with your heavenly parents, you were well educated and comforted as to your ability and chances of success. They were by far in your favor. Your heavenly parents loved you so much that they were not going to allow you to have an experience in which you would not be successful. Their confidence in you and your abilities was great.

When your opportunity to talk with your heavenly parents about your experiences on earth arrived, you were very excited. All you wanted was to get there and have your turn. You could see the end from the beginning; you knew the outcome of your experience. You knew where the education would take you and the outcome you would eventually achieve if you followed their guidelines. You were very excited about the plan.

Imagine now that it is time to talk to your heavenly parents about your turn on earth. Let's create a scenario of the conversation to give you a better understanding of what happened then.

———————————————————————————————

Both of your heavenly parents are present, and your Heavenly Father begins to speak.

"Hello, my sweet child. Are you ready for your experience on earth?"

"Yes, Father. I am so excited and so grateful for this opportunity, and I feel so blessed to have you as my guide and to have your constant help available to me while I am there. I know it will be a very different experience than our home here, but I am excited and ready to go. I have a lot of preparations to make before it is my turn. So can we get started?"

"Certainly, dear," your mother says. "That is why you are here. Today we are going to spiritually create your experience on earth. You know everything is created spiritually first, right?"

"Yes, I remember that."

"Well, this is what you are going to do today. You have watched the creation of the earth unfold, and you have been taught the creation process in school. You did very well on your lessons. Now it is time for you to actually create your life. Have you considered what you want?"

"Oh, yes, I have, and I am so excited about the outcome. I think the most significant thing I want is to be like you and Father. I want whatever I do to bring me back into your presence. I know that is everyone's eventual goal, but I am really determined to be at your side when I am finished. I want to be just like you. I love you so much."

"That is wonderful, my sweet. We love you that much and more. As you know our love is eternal."

"Yes, knowing that makes me really happy."

"Okay, dear, let's move on with our planning. What else do you want?"

"First, I have a question. I have been watching those who have gone before and observing their experiences, and I don't understand how they are going to get back. It seems like so many of them are lost and don't remember you. How do they make it back?"

"Well, that has all been worked out. I'll let Father introduce the entire plan so that you can better understand the process."

Father begins to speak. "You seem pretty excited. Shall we just get started?"

"Oh, yes, I am so excited! I just want to get there and be on my mission."

"Okay, then, here is how it works. We will start your mission here in the spiritual realm. You will now be given many opportunities to watch others who have gone before you to learn from them. You will see what they have done well, and from this experience you will then choose what you want for your experiences."

At this point our student spends time watching those who are having and have had their life experiences. Not only does the student watch the experiences, but the student is also privileged to see the eventual outcome of those experiences. The student watches for a very long time and then, when ready, returns to Father for further instruction.

"Father, I believe I am ready for the next step. I have studied my predecessors and have watched their growth, and I think I know what I want for my experience."

"Very well. Let's hear it."

"I know the first and most important thing for my experience is to have you in my life. I want to always be close to you and always turn to you. My intention is to return with honor and to be successful at everything I have chosen. I intend to make it back into your presence and to live with you again. Father, I have a great many items on my list. I have many things I want to do while I am there. Is that okay?"

"Certainly, dear. You can have any experience you want, and you can have as much as you want. It will all be encoded within when you are ready."

"I have a lot on my list. Do you want to see my goals?"

"Yes, let's." (Father reviews the goals.) "My, my. That is quite a long list. I know you can do it all if you stay focused."

He then continues, "Let's see, you want to lead people to Christ; you want to heal like the Savior does. You want to be gifted in many foreign languages and restore an ancient language. Now that is an interesting goal. You want to be a mother and raise your children up in righteousness; you want to be like Father Joseph and interpret dreams. You want to be a writer and write books that will last through the generations of time. You want to follow the living prophets of the day. You want to have a strong and constant relationship with the Savior. You want to bear testimony of Him during your entire sojourn on earth. You want to experience many of your favorite places that you have seen on the earth, which means you will be traveling all over the earth. You want to be a teacher of sacred principles and a leader among your fellow man. You want to teach new principles, things that have not yet been revealed or are on the forefront of the times. You want to write stories that teach as the Savior did, in parables. You want to be an excellent orator, and you want to be an example of the believers. You want to have a healthy marriage and be a strong woman of faith. You want to be a conscious creator, and you want to witness and experience miracles. You want to live your life as close to the life of the Savior as you possibly can. You want to change the planet."

He pauses. "Now what do you mean by that? Do you want the earth to be oval instead of round?" Father chuckles.

"No, I mean I want my life to have an effect for good. I really want to make a difference while I am there."

"Oh, okay. Well, dear, you are right; this is a very long list, and we are only halfway through it. You have been busy."

"Yes, I have watched everyone for a very long time. I figured I could since I would not be going down for some time."

"Very well, then. Let's move on."

(Father continues to read and soon finishes the list.)

"Do feel your list is complete?"

"Well … it is as complete as I can make it, but I am always open for suggestions. If you have anything that you think would be important, that perhaps I have forgotten, could we add it to the list?"

"Certainly, dear, and thank you, because there are a few things I personally would like you to do while you are there. I will simply add them to the bottom of the list, and you can ponder them for a while and see how you feel about the additions. If you are okay with them, we will leave them. Later, if you want to change or remove them, we can do that too. After all, it is your life."

"Oh, no, Father. I want to do whatever you want me to do. I will do them."

"Did you even look at them?"

"No, but I know you, and I know you would never give me anything that is not for my good."

"Thank you for your sweet faith, dear. You still might want to look at them."

"Oh, Father, that is big. That's a very big job! Do you think I could do that along with my list?"

"Yes, dear. I know you very well. I know what you are capable of."

"Well, okay then. I will do it."

After you chose your life experiences (and this is a condensed version of the process; it lasted for a very significant amount of time), you began to look at each event and learn the process involved in making those experiences come about.

When you began this part of the process, you became very excited; you knew you would be able to have an enormous number of experiences. At this point, you knew what you would experience, and you knew the extent of the opposition you needed to experience to learn all that you needed to learn to bring your desired goals to fruition.

Once a goal was set, you were taught the process of achieving that goal. For instance, once you made the decision to heal like the Savior, *illness* was added to your experience list because, in order to learn the healing arts, you needed the experience of illness yourself. A physician who had never experienced pain or illness would have little understanding of the condition his patients were in and little compassion for them and their experience.

In order to become what you wanted to become, you needed to experience the opposite to gain the knowledge to be what you wanted to be. That was the entire plan; you were going to experience the world of opposition.

In order to be a great leader, you would need to experience situations in your life in which you understood and were aware of the need for good leadership and could be taught the importance of leadership talents and skills. For everything you wanted, you needed schooling to achieve it. You needed life events to be placed within your plan to help you get to the desired goals. This little gal had a great deal on her list, and because of that she would need to experience a great deal of opposition in order to achieve her desired goals. She had a lot to learn.

When you chose what you wanted to become, Father then facilitated it by setting up life situations to help you achieve that desired goal. For instance, if you wanted to help the poor, he would put you in situations that would line you up for that experience. Your life events would lead you to that end. The family you were born into, the country you initially lived in—everything would be in alignment to give you the maximum experience to help you achieve that end. Heavenly Father helped extensively with this process. From God's place of omniscience (all-knowing), He knew just what you needed to achieve the goals you desired.

After your goals were set and Father set up your life circumstances to help you achieve them, the entire process was reviewed, and then a contract was made between you and God. The contract said that you agreed with the plan, that this was what you wanted, and that this was what you intended to achieve while you were in your second estate, or on earth. Once the contract was signed and agreed upon, Father then set up a system in your body that would help you toward your desired goals.

Certain contracts would open at specific times in your life, and then events would follow that would lead you to that end. Your contracts were set within your DNA in the form of vibrations. When you experienced particular events and reached specific vibrations, the contracts would respond to the vibration and would begin to open and lead you to your desired goal. People and events would come into your life that would enable you to remember the desires of your heart. You would feel a longing to make something happen. You would feel a longing to study medicine or languages or to travel. Whatever was set within your contracts, your heart would lead you to the fulfillment of those dreams and plans.

Perhaps you are feeling a longing to move forward in life, but you are stopped because of your life's events. You can't seem to figure out which way to go. You feel a huge desire to move, but you also feel stuck in many areas. When this occurs, it causes great conflict within.

The reason life feels the way it does is that it is time to move forward into new contracts, but you are still stuck with the old ones playing out. You have not gotten the lesson they are trying to teach you, and your new contracts are loudly knocking at your door, ready for you to get moving on them. This situation will amplify the opposition in your life.

You set up your life's events, you chose what you wanted to experience, and you chose the number of goals you wanted to accomplish. You looked very carefully over the plan, and you agreed with Father that you would complete them. This is the life you wanted. The problem now is that you have forgotten that you made such agreements; you have forgotten what your contracts are, and you have forgotten how you are to move forward into them.

It is time to change. It is time to awaken to the fact that you have made spiritual contracts and that you are on the road to fulfilling them. When you accept this fact and then have a desire to get on with your life, you can begin to move very intentionally forward, like you intended in the beginning.

There are very specific things that will help you move forward in your contracts. There is a way to find out what your contracts are. You can know and remember your life's plan, if this is what you want.

Knowing my spiritual contracts has certainly helped me understand my life's events in a most profound way. When

I began to understand my spiritual contracts and have them restored to my memory, everything I have gone through began to make perfect sense. I have struggled with being overweight my entire life; I have done everything one could imagine to help myself, but nothing budged the weight. I went to the Lord over and over again to help me with this problem. I spent a lot of time on my knees trying to get over it, trying to discover just what I needed to do. The conventional methods never seemed to work for me. Then the magical day arrived when I learned why this situation was in my life, why I had experienced such great opposition because of it. I learned what it was to teach me.

One of the most significant and important goals and contracts that I had made—in fact, it was the first contract I made—was that I would always be close to Heavenly Father. This was the most significant thing on my list; it was the most important goal to me. So Heavenly Father, in His wisdom, placed a situation in my life that would create great opposition. He knew the time I would be on the earth. It was a time when the shape of the physical body was extremely important to people; there would be an obsession with having a thin and perfect body. He knew that if I were to experience the opposite, the plague of the generation, then I would spend a great deal of time praying for help. This situation would contribute to our closeness. He also placed other very trying events in my life to help achieve this end. I was placed in an abusive home; I had an abusive father, and my mother was a woman of great faith. This combination gave me the background I needed to have the faith and the relationship with Heavenly Father that I wanted. It was all perfect.

Every event in our lives can teach us and provide us the outcome of our desired goals. If we had a desire to be an individual of great faith, then we would be placed in situations that would help us achieve that end. We would experience great fear and have opportunities that would expose us to the building of faith. Every single event in your life has purpose.

Do you know what the purpose is? Do you know why you have the challenges you do? Do you know what the intention of each opposition experience is?

Each and every opposition experience we have is to teach and help us gain knowledge.

Remember that the fall of Adam and Eve came about because they partook of the fruit of the tree of knowledge of good and evil. That one action brought them into this experience. They came to gain knowledge. We are here to gain knowledge and experience.

So now what? Here you are, completely loaded with goals you created for yourself in your first estate, or in the premortal life. You are experiencing great opposition. We learned in the first few chapters of this book that the reason we are now experiencing such great opposition is that we have not let go of our early misconceptions about life. We learned that when a misconception is frozen in us, it is frozen in the form of vibration. When these vibrations are activated by a life experience (a trigger moment), they rise to the surface in an effort to get our attention and to bring the misconception into resolution. Once the thought is brought into resolution, the misconception is naturalized and will no longer cause us opposition. We have these misconceptions to give us experience, but once we experience the opposition they are intended to bring into our life, we can at any point after the experience bring them into resolution. (For more information about trigger moments, refer to Chapter 15.)

Our spiritual contracts are connected to this. We came here to learn a great deal and to have a great many experiences. Not all of our experiences were intended to be painful ones. The little girl in our example wanted to travel and experience the beauties of the earth and to speak many languages fluently; this does not have to be a painful experience. Yet, in achieving these goals, it would be helpful if they were known by the individual who made the contracts.

What do you want to do in life that you have never been able to achieve? Do you have a longing in your heart to accomplish a great goal that you have not the faintest idea how you are going to bring about? Have you always wanted to travel, write, or create something? Or perhaps have you desired to be a dancer but are disabled, or you have a desire to invent something but don't know how you are even going to get the supplies or knowledge to accomplish such a thing. The longings in your heart are your contracts at work. They are pulling you to your desired goals.

What do you dream of? What do you want? How do you discover what your contracts are? Can we know this information or do we just have to walk by faith the whole way, never knowing, only taking a step at a time?

When I discovered my contract to be close to Heavenly Father and realized that the way to fulfill it was by experiencing obesity, I became instantly grateful for obesity. I had no regrets. I wept for joy in gratitude for my heavy body. Because of obesity, I now have a very intimate and personal relationship with God; I can talk to Him every day. I can get my every question answered on the spot. The gift this trial bestowed was by far greater than the trial itself. I know I would do it again in a heartbeat, which is why I agreed in a contract to do it in the first place. You see, that is the way with God. For any personal challenge we go through in an effort to achieve or reach our goals, God has provided the outcome to outweigh the effort a million fold. Can you imagine anything more valuable than a personal, close relationship with God, a relationship in which you spend time with Him, laugh with Him, and feel His love, His gentle arms around you on a daily basis? In my estimation, going through this huge trial was worth every bit of it. I wanted this outcome with all of my heart; I got it and am grateful for it.

In my past, no matter what I did to lose weight, it never worked for me. It wouldn't. I was programmed to keep the weight on until I reached the desired closeness with God. I could not lose weight until my relationship had reached the point where it is now. I knew in the beginning what I wanted, and God programmed me to that end. I then agreed to it by signing the contract. I agreed to have this experience, and I am so grateful for it.

Once you discover your contracts, you will understand your life in an extremely significant way. Everything will begin to make sense. You will know why you were never able to get past that huge trial: you hadn't learned everything the trial had to teach you. You hadn't fulfilled the contract. If a trial is still present in your life, you can ask what you need to know and do in order to fulfill the contract so you can finally be done with it. It can be pretty simple from here on out.

At this point, you might be wondering how to discover what your contracts are. The only way to discover your contracts is through personal revelation. You begin with a desire to know what they are, and then you ask God to reveal them to you. You specifically ask to have the memory of your contracts restored to you. Everything you need to know is within; it is only a prayer away. It is as simple as discovering that you have a great new file on your computer. You simply double-click on it to open the file. Your contract file is already downloaded into your DNA, and all you need to do to get it to open is simply ask for it. Once you have asked to know what is in your contract file, you then prepare yourself for the information.

You prepare by first getting connected with your guidance system. Your guidance system is the way into your spiritual contracts. Once you are able to clearly discern messages from your guidance system, you will be able to know what your spiritual contracts are.

Some of you at this point might be thinking, *That is a ways away. I have a lot to learn before I can get this information.* But it need not be. We are moving at a very fast rate these days. Things are changing at lightning speed, and so are you.

Learning to connect with your guidance system is as simple as paying attention to the way you feel. Become conscious of your life. Let the way you feel take top billing on your focus list. Nothing should be more important than the way you feel. Once you begin to become cognizant of the way you feel, listen to your guidance system, and begin to heed its signals, you will be in alignment to hear the whisperings of the Spirit, the voice of God. You will be turning your focus inward, which is where the Spirit dwells. All of your communications will come from within. Even the voice of God will be heard and discerned from within. When you attune yourself to your guidance system, which is internal, you will then be in a great position to hear the voice of God. You will be able to get all of your questions answered and soon will know exactly what your contracts are, what you are to learn, and how you are to move forward in them.

I have helped clients learn about their spiritual contracts, but the best way is to learn to discover them on your own. You have many contracts; they are programmed to open at different times throughout your life. Wouldn't it be wonderful to have the ability to ask your questions as they come up and not have to worry about trying to find someone to help you with them?

I love my communications with God. I love my relationship with Him; I love having the freedom to ask Him anything and learn the answers for myself. It's awesome. I ask Him not only about my spiritual contracts but about absolutely everything else I have a need to know. The only thing required on my part is time. I need to take the time to listen to the answers. It does take time, especially the way I do it. I always write both the question and the answer so I can stay in remembrance of what I want to know. In the beginning, when I was learning to communicate with God, writing helped me stay focused. It is easy to let your mind wander, or at least it was for me.

I feel I am still a baby in this. I know I have a ways to go in my personal relationship with God, but I am on my way. I am so grateful for the contract that I made that enabled me to develop this closeness. I am so grateful for obesity; it was the way to that end.

Spiritual Contracts

A Personal Experience

The following piece is a selection from my journal, written after I discovered my spiritual contract with obesity.

_____

"Heavenly Father, can I lose the weight now? Have I fulfilled the contract?"

"Not quite, Tannie. There is one more thing to do to fulfill this contract."

"Can I know what that is?"

"Certainly, dear. All you have to do to fulfill the contract is to write a long list of all that you have been able to experience because of your heavy body. You are going to write the list for your readers so they can see the gift of their opposition. This you will put in your book at the end of the spiritual contract piece."

"Then will the contract be fulfilled?"

"Yes, my dear. It will be fulfilled."

"Father, what do we do when a contract is fulfilled?"

"You get to check it off your list of things to do."

"Well, that sounds great. I love getting things done. Anything else?"

"Yes. The knowledge of the experience is cemented into your being as the gift of the experience. You will always have that knowledge to draw upon for your future life experiences. You will have the gift of the experience. Now as you go through life, when you need the closeness and love we agreed to when you completed the contract, you will have it available to you."

"Thank you, Father. Anything else?"

"No. Let's write the piece on spiritual contracts. You are going to love it."

"Cool. Let's go. I am ready."

_____

I then wrote the above piece about spiritual contracts.

Completing My Spiritual Contract with Obesity

The Gift of My Opposition

The most significant gift bestowed upon me as a result of my heavy body was the development of a close personal relationship with God. I have spent a lot of time in prayer with Him, praying about my body and the way I felt physically.

I have learned a lot about nutrition and the operations and function of the body because of obesity. I have learned a lot about herbs. I learned how to identify them, gather them from nature, and make my own herbal combinations and medicines. I learned how to cook everything from scratch—how to sprout, solar cook, and grow and harvest wheat grass. I learned how to make flourless bread, grind flour, and take some really bitter medicine without tossing my cookies. I learned how to doctor my children because of all I was learning. They never went to the doctor when they were little. I was Dr. Mom. I even helped the neighbors with their family needs. I learned about depression.

I learned how to sew when I was nine and sewed most of my own clothes through high school and part of college because I had a belief that it was difficult to buy clothes in my size. Because I had developed the ability to sew, I made some of my mother's clothes, which was a great gift to her. I was the only child to ever do that for her. I learned to look my best whenever I got ready for the day. I paid attention to fashion and did my best to stay up with it, even at my size. I learned that skinny people have a hard time buying clothes too; I was shocked when I learned that one.

I learned that you could have a great time with your friends even if you didn't have a date to the Valentine's dance. I learned compassion for those who are different because of the judgment I experienced because of my size. I learned that there are only two types of people in the world: those you love and those you don't understand. I learned to forgive rude people quickly, knowing they did not understand me or my situation. I learned to be patient for those who were slow and had a difficult time moving. I learned compassion for those who hurt all the time. I learned to rub people's feet and massage places they couldn't reach because it felt so good, especially if they were overweight or disabled. I learned that movement is very important to life.

I learned that being overweight has nothing to do with finding love and getting married; it is your belief in yourself that matters. I learned how to do things in unconventional ways because of my body. I learned that saying unkind things to others can be as hurtful as a punch in the face. Faces mend easier than hearts. I learned that children love soft moms. I learned to never judge others; we don't know what their contracts are.

I learned to love those who are difficult to love; I learned to serve in a far greater capacity than I would have had I not been heavy. I learned to make my moments count. I learned everything I know that is in my course books and in my volumes and volumes of journals. I learned a lot about God and my life with Him before I came. I learned how to heal my life God's way and how to teach others to do the same.

I learned how to read energy. I learned about my spiritual gifts. I learned to genuinely forgive and to do so quickly. I learned to appreciate inventive people who make life easier for the physically challenged. I learned that 90 percent of handicapped-accessible bathrooms are questionably designed— the toilet is very high and the paper is near the floor. I learned to be a creative and fun mom. I enjoyed a lot of movies. I learned that diets don't work because you are always focused on weight, on what is wrong with you, not your perfection and what you are doing right.

This is only a partial list. I am sure that if I spent more time on it, I could come up with a zillion more things I have learned and that I am grateful for. This little piece was simply written off the top of my head.

I am grateful for all that I have learned because of the gift of my heavy body.

Being grateful for your opposition is the final step in any contract. When you can express genuine gratitude for your opposition, the contract is fulfilled.

Part II
How to Initiate Change

13

Initiate the Change Sequence Now

Life is filled with mystery. Do you understand why you think the way you do or why you respond to people and events the way you do?

For most of us, the biggest mystery in life is trying to understand ourselves. For the first half of our lives, we are very good at pointing our fingers outward, thinking the pain we feel must be caused by outside forces. I mean, after all, "they" are the ones who inflict pressure and pain upon us, so indeed our pain must be everyone else's fault. Right? For a significant portion of our life we have the tendency to blame others for our pain and misfortune. But eventually the magic day arrives when we realize that the only person we really have any say or control over is ourselves. So if we don't want to feel the heat and the pain anymore, we must remove ourselves from the fire.

We try removing ourselves from the fire and pain we feel in many ways: we get a divorce, we quit our jobs, we move out of the neighborhood, we leave our families, and we enter new relationships, always with the hope that this "big change" is what we need to reach our desired goals, to attain the desires of our heart, which usually are peace, joy, and happiness. When we make these significant changes, life seems to get better at first because we have interrupted our patterns, but when we become comfortable in our new surroundings, the familiar begins to creep in. We again begin to develop the same problems we experienced before, only this time there is a new twist on them—but in truth it's the same. Totally frustrated, we cry out, "Why can't I do this? What is wrong with me? Why can't I make the changes I really want to make? Why can't I just be at peace? Why doesn't life work for me? I see others happy. What is wrong with me? Why can't I make it to that 'happy place'? Am I destined to live my life in misery and pain? What did I ever do wrong? Why do bad things always happen to me?"

You have heard the question, "Why do bad things happen to good people?" Well, in truth, bad things happen to bad people too, but if you are trying to be really good and bad things happen, it feels like God is slapping you in the face. "Why?" you wonder, and you again ask, "What am I doing wrong?"

You aren't really doing anything wrong. What you are doing is growing into the masterpiece you intended in the beginning. Everything that happens in your life happens for one reason. Whether you are good or bad, all of our life events happen for one simple reason: to bring us growth.

We came into this realm to progress and to grow, which you are doing each and every day of your life. If we were to stop growing we would become unsatisfied, because within we are encoded to progress and move ever forward. The motivating force behind our growth is our opposition. It is our pain and all the little annoyances and problems we face daily that bring us the growth we need. This is the divine pattern of growth. If we did not have anything to overcome, we would stop growing, and this is not what a great, eternal being wants to do. You are on your way to greatness, and you would be very unhappy if you stopped short of that goal. That's what it means to be damned—being stopped in your progression.

You will never stop because deep within is a divinely encoded program that keeps you moving forward to help you attain your full potential.

What is your full potential?

You are a child of God, and your full potential is to become like your eternal parents.

You are a seedbed of greatness. I believe you know that. At times, you have felt deep within a desire to do something great and wonderful. This is your heritage; you were born for greatness. Perhaps you are wondering, "Can we all be great? Can everyone make it to the top? If someone is on top, then someone has to be on the bottom. We can't all be winners. That's just not how life is."

That is our limited way of seeing things, but God did not intend for some of His children to not make it so others could look better and be more successful than the rest. That is simply not the way of God. Think of your own family, your own children. Do you want only one or two to be successful while not caring what happens to the rest of them? Certainly not! You want each one to make it to the top; you want each child to be who he or she is destined to be. Father in Heaven did not send any of us down here to fail. He did not send us down here to get stuck; He sent us here to complete our mission, move on, and become like He is.

God said, "For behold, this is my work and my glory to bring to pass the immortality and eternal life of man." (Pearl of Great Price | Moses 1:39)

If God's work and glory is to bring you to His high, exalted station, then don't you think that would be included in your life's plan? Don't you think it would really be what your life was all about?

It certainly would. You don't start your work of becoming great when you can get a handle on your life. You began that glorifying process the day you were born, and you are actively involved in that process every day of your life. Don't think that because your life is hard, somehow you are doing something wrong.

News flash!

Every day, you are working and moving toward perfection, immortality, and eternal life. This is part of your heritage as a child of God. Think about it. *Every day,* you are at work. Did you even know that? All of the aches, pains, mistakes, woes, troubles, drama, psychotic episodes, breakdowns, and depression are evidence of you happily at work, becoming the masterpiece you intended to be in the beginning.

Perhaps you are wondering, "How can that be? How can I be working toward immortality and perfection when life is so awful and all I want is for the ride to end and the pain to stop?"

Well, if you are ready for the pain to stop, then you are ready for the joy to begin. You are ready to enter the second phase of your earth experience. The first phase is to experience opposition; the second phase is to invite peace.

We can have peace anytime we are ready for it, but it will take training and a bit of thought time to initiate the sequence that brings forth this experience.

How Do You Begin to Bring Forth Peace?

The first step is to recognize our misconceptions about life. When we realize that we are right on course and don't really need to do anything but simply move forward from here that offers us great relief.

Once you understand that we are all programmed with opposition, you can then do what it takes to change your programming.

The process looks something like this. Each day, as you experience negative emotion, you stop and discover where it is coming from or why you are having this experience in your life. If you desire to change it, you do so right then and there.

It is like keeping your physical house clean. Doing a little each day makes the work light. However, sometimes we still choose to do major spring cleaning projects and sometimes we need to call in professional help, but it is all good.

Some of our life's opposition experiences can feel so big that we will want help getting to it and through it, which is okay. I personally have had a lot of help with my internal cleaning and clearing needs. There were patterns so ingrained in my DNA that I needed the professionals to help get them out. Each time I did a "big project," I was grateful for the help. Whenever I had a big internal cleaning project to do, I always had someone with me. God knew I needed help, and help arrived in perfect timing. This is the magic of this work. It is always perfect. All you have to do is simply trust your heart.

When your heart leads, it will always lead you with the feeling of "This is what I want and/or need to do." If ever you were to resist your heart's desires, then outside forces would show up to get your attention, to help get you to the place you need to be.

Once, I received an invitation to a particular course in my field of study. I didn't really want to go, but after I had received three invitations to the same event, I thought, *Maybe I should take another look at this.* I was grateful I did. It was one of the biggest clearing experiences of my life.

The magic of changing your life begins with the key of desire. When the desire to change is put in place, changes will naturally begin to transpire. People and events will come into your life to get you to the place you desire most to go, and then in time you will obtain the desires of your heart.

I think one of my personal shortcomings was in the area of patience. Once I began this work, I wanted to complete it quickly. It felt so good to change after not knowing how for so long. Once you begin the change process, you are on a wonderful road of discovery.

The next step in the change process is an instruction I received from the Spirit. I was told to ask more questions. That one stumped me. I was told to ask questions, yet I didn't know what questions to ask.

I know that asking questions is a significant key to getting answers. I first asked to know the questions I was to ask. Then it all began to slowly sink in. Now I ask questions in prayer every day. I have a notebook handy to write down the things I want to know. Many times during the day, things will happen that I don't understand, and so I'll jot my questions down in my little book. Then, when I have the time to pray, I pull out my notebook and go over one question at a time. I pray my question prayers while I am on the computer; these are my journal entries, my online chat time with God. In this way, when the Spirit answers, I have a record of the questions and the answers. I then have them to refer to later on when I ask the same question again. I have done this many times. I have needed to hear the same answer multiple times before I understood what I was being taught. Also, when the Spirit speaks to your heart, sometimes it is so beautiful and you feel so loved that you want to remember the experience. So if you are in a practice of recording your questions and answers, soon you will have your own sacred script of conversations with God.

In summary, the first step is having a desire to change and trusting you are on your path. Whether you know it or not, you will be led to where you need to go.

Then ask questions and record them and the answers. You can learn a great deal about yourself, your friends, your family, your work, and your purpose as you connect to God and begin to trust the answers that come to you.

Remember that any negative thought or experience can be changed. This is what it means to be a child of God. You have the power to alter your universe and your experience. You have the power to change the very fabric that your life tapestry is composed of. In the past, it was woven with threads of pain.

Now and in the future, it will be woven with threads of gold as you discover the mystery and majesty of being the divine child that you are.

You will never know of your greatness unless you have a desire to discover this part of yourself. You will never understand your life and the purpose of it until you have a desire to ask questions with a true intent of having your questions answered.

You have the power to understand the greatest mysteries of life. You have the power to understand yourself and how and why you relate to the world the way you do. Begin to use this power by taking your first step on the road to change. Seize the moment now. There is no better time than the present to receive the gift your personal life has to offer the world. Begin today to experience a mighty change of heart.

14

And It Came to Pass

We have had years of experience feeling negative emotions, yet few of us really know what we are to do with them. Because we have lacked this knowledge, we tend to do what those who have gone before us have done. We stuff them, push them away, and generally don't deal with them, but it is by "dealing" with our negative emotions that our greatest purpose is discovered. Once we understand what the negative emotions and experiences are to teach us, we can move on and become more of who we are intended to be. It is going through these experiences that will give us the gift of our time here on earth. Allow me to share a personal experience that provided insight into my life, the purpose of negative emotion, and the principle of letting go.

My Journal, June 26, 2005

I have had a most interesting Sunday, one in which I have learned a great deal. My lesson began on my way to church. As I was walking through the doors, I became very ill. I went straight into the bathroom. I felt my insides churn and jab; my head ached. I decided that I was just going to be with the pain, allow it, and breathe through it. In doing so, I had a very interesting dream/vision about pain.

I saw in my mind's eye my house, and pain came knocking at the door. He was very scary, dressed completely in black. I opened the door and let him in. He rushed into my house, and I panicked. I shoved and locked him in a closet because I did not know what to do with him. I left him there and went about my day's work, always knowing he was there. I kept him in the closet for a very long time. I could hear him pounding and beating around in the closet. He wanted out. He scared me so badly that I didn't dare let him out. I did not know what he wanted or why he had come or what he would do if I let him out.

There were times life went relatively well because I had turned my focus to other areas and I forgot about him. But then there were times that I became very aware of him. Man, he was really bugging me. I wanted him out, but I was afraid of him and what he would do.

I got tired of him, and so one day I let him out. He merely went out the back door.

I then saw a different scenario.

I saw pain knocking at my door. I let him in; I was not afraid. He took his hand and touched my body, going all the way around, just running his fingers around me as if I were a spindle. Then, when the circle was complete, he left out the back door as quickly as he had come in. He had come to merely give me the experience of his presence.

I realized then how, because of fear, I had kept pain in my house (my body) because I was too afraid of what he would do if I let him out.

His intention was to give me experience and to pass through. He never intended to stay. I was the one who kept him locked in my closet, fearful of his presence in my life.

Each time a new pain came to my door, I responded the same way until my house was full of pain and began to break down under the load. Years ago when my house could contain no more and I faced death, I turned to Heavenly Father and prayed, "Father, I need help. I need a core change. I can't manage all that is in my house. I am full of pain, and I can't move."

Then in that instant, the heavens responded. I saw in my mind's eye a group of angels roll up their sleeves, and one announced to the others, "She is ready. Let's go." I didn't understand at the time why they were rolling up their sleeves. All I wanted was the pain to leave my life. Now as the years have passed, along with experience I have gained understanding. They were rolling up their sleeves because they were coming to help me clean my house. They were going to teach me how to let go of the pain. My house is cleaner now, and I am in joy.

Today as I write this I want you to know I am still working on my house; I had a lot of pain stuffed in there. I, through the process of time, became very creative in where I stored it. I suppose my heavenly crew could have taken care of it much quicker. In fact, at one point I asked them why they hadn't. I was told that being the kind of person who likes to know how things work, I chose to go this way so I could learn just how it did work. If I would have had the pain removed in an instant, I would have been questioning, "Now how does that work, and why did you do that?" Father, knowing me, took me this way so I could learn how to clean house heaven's way. In truth this is really what I wanted to learn—how to heal my life and be free of pain, God's way.

It has been a fruitful journey. Now when pain comes knocking at my door—and it still does at times, like today—I invite it in. I am not afraid of it anymore. I simply ask, "What is wanted? What is your purpose in coming? What am I to learn from this visit?" Quickly I get the answer, and quickly pain passes through, as it did today.

Now I can live each day feeling free and joyful. I no longer fear the lesson. Now pain is my gifted teacher and friend, and I am grateful for its presence in my life.

If I had never experienced his presence, I would never have felt this kind of joy because it was from pain passing through that I learned how to live and be in joy.

15

The Intent and Purpose of Negative Emotion

Feeling Your Misconceptions Rise to the Surface

Do you have people in your life who push your buttons? Or situations and events that trigger in you exaggerated negative emotion? Do you know why this happens or what to do when it happens?

All matter in its finest element is energy. When you feel any emotion, you are feeling energy in motion. We have experienced many emotions in our lives—some positive, some negative. We prefer the positive, but it is important to understand that both have a purpose and both are important.

When you feel negative emotion, it causes movement of some kind. *The intent and purpose of all negative emotions is to produce change, to promote growth, and to provide experience.* We have had many years experiencing these negative emotions. Now it is time to learn from our negative experiences quickly so we can move on and live our lives in joy.

My intention in presenting this information is to teach you how to use your negative emotions to quickly make movement, understand the lessons, and then change the negative experience into a positive one and have joy.

As you experience this work and as you go through life, there will be times that negative feelings are triggered in you. If this occurs, it is good. You will have just discovered a jackpot of energy. This is the very spot you will begin to learn the lesson that the negative experience is intended to teach you.

Throughout this work, you will learn how to turn negative perceptions and experiences into positive experiences, which will facilitate your movement into joy. This is what living in joy is all about—using negative energy in a positive way. So if negative emotions are triggered and rise to the top, it's good; you are on your way. You will be taught ways to move on and through them quickly. We learn and change, learn and change, until the day arrives that we are able to stay in a high joy vibration.

What Is a Trigger, and Why Are We Triggered?

When we are triggered (the equivalent of getting our buttons pushed), we experience exaggerated, strong negative emotions and feelings. It is caused from a present stimuli; a smell, a sound, an event, a song, a person, a word, an inflection of a word, or a phrase, which connects to a past cellular memory, usually a trauma of some kind.

For example, consider the following:

- Upon hearing a car backfire, I would feel agitated and afraid ... *because in my past I used to have to duck so I wouldn't get hit by stray bullets.*
- When I became tired, I felt I had to keep going, always pushing myself to exhaustion ... *because one evening when I was young, my mom and I were working and I was very tired—I just wanted to go to bed—but Mom said, "You can't stop until the job is done." I believed her.*

- When I went for a drive in the woods, I became panicked and fearful ... *because it reminded me of the time I was abducted.*
- When someone raises his or her voice, I want to run away ... *because it reminds me of my parents fighting and yelling when I was little.*
- All throughout my life, I had to do everything myself even though I really wanted help ... *because when I was born I felt panicked and cut off, believing I was on my own.*
- When I would shop for meat, it always made me queasy ... *because when I was little I watched my father gut a deer, and I swore I would never eat that because it was yucky.*
- When my husband would leave to go anywhere on Sundays, I would always get very mad, even if he was attending a church meeting ... *because when I was little my mom used to take us all to church by herself while my dad went to visit another woman. My mom knew what he was doing, and it made her so mad. So I learned that when Dad leaves on Sunday, you get mad.*

When we are triggered and feel or observe a negative pattern, we usually know only the first half of the story (the roman type). We feel the strong negative emotion or irritating pattern, and the rest of the story (*the italic type*) is hidden from our view, lurking somewhere in our cellular memory, our hearts, or our subconscious minds. When we connect the two parts and get a new perception and picture, we experience resolution and change.

This is the object of our clearing techniques, imageries, and sessions. Our intention is to connect the strong negative emotions to our core subconscious belief. Once the core cellular memory is discovered and brought to the surface with the intention to resolve or release it, it will be so, thus enabling you to become the master of your thoughts and life.

These negative patterns and beliefs have purpose. They are there to cause movement and growth and to provide experience in opposition. The good news here is that once we have the experience we came to learn from, we are then able to move forward, bringing the misconception, negative perception, and core beliefs into alignment with our positive mind change.

This positive life change can happen any time during our experience here upon the earth. The only thing required for change is the desire to change and recognition of the problem. We can't change any part of our lives without first seeing the need. Most of us are about changing everyone else first because their patterns and behaviors are so easy to see. What we don't realize is that the reason those behaviors are so easily recognized is because these same energy offerings and patterns are resonating inside of us as well. This is called the mirror principle (which is also illustrated in Chapter 31 in the story "Mirror Mirror").

You live in a reflective universe. The behaviors you see in others are there to help you discover the misconceptions inside yourself.

Here is an example of the mirror principle: One day, three neighbor children came over to play with my children. Normally, these children were delightful and fun to have around, but on this particular day they were really bugging me. I felt agitated and annoyed. Feeling this and having worked this process for some time, I separated myself to find answers and achieve resolution. I first began to question what was happening, why I was feeling these strong negative feelings, and then I prayed for enlightenment. As soon as I set the intention to discover the core of my discomfort a sweet knowing came to me. I had three whiny children (inner child traumas or misconceptions) inside of me that needed attention and resolution. This knowledge brought great joy. My next step was to set the intention during my next session to connect to the three children (a cellular memory), meet their needs, and bring the experience into resolution and healing. I did so with joy.

It was wonderful. The next time the three children came over, I enjoyed their sweet presence and did not have to experience the previous negative agitation.

These children had frequented my home over a few years, but it was not until I was ready that this information surfaced. I then chose to look at it and bring the discomfort this situation caused in me into resolution. In doing so, the negative experience and feelings triggered by their presence left my life for good. The agitation had nothing to do with the children; it was all about me.

Our disharmonies and core cellular memories are like slivers in our souls. They often surface, trying to get our attention. What we don't understand is that this discomfort is a message of desired resolution and healing. So what do we typically do? We often push the sliver back in, thinking that somehow this is a part of us and it belongs deep inside. It doesn't belong inside. It was there to give you experience in opposition, causing discomfort and growth, but it can be plucked out anytime you are ready. Remember that the original intention is to give you experience. Once you have had the experience, you can at any time pull the sliver out. Even your physical body models this for you by systematically pushing a sliver to the surface to be removed. This is the same pattern our inner intelligence uses to help us cleanse our inner vessels and move us to a place of peace, harmony, and balance. We are programmed to have all impurities pushed to the surface in an effort to get our attention. If we have understanding and knowledge, we will choose to pull the sliver out. Because this information has never been presented quite like this, most of us have spent our days medicating ourselves and pushing all the garbage back in, never realizing how great it feels to get it out and let it go. You know how relieved you feel to get an annoying sliver out of your skin. Imagine how great it would feel to get a giant belief that you are worthless, alone, and not good enough removed. From experience I can tell you, as can any of my clients, that letting go of negative core beliefs and patterns is a great experience and one that truly brings joy.

The hardest thing for most beginning students is separating themselves from their experiences. Once they catch a glimpse of what is in there, they feel shame for having it in there in the first place. This pattern of thinking does not serve us. We are here to gain experience in opposition and to use our gift of agency to move through it.

Christ passed through opposition. He passed through severe opposition, but you don't look at Him as being anything less than who He is, the Son of God.

You too are a child of God and are here to experience opposition, but your experience does not define your true divine nature. Let the cup pass; don't hold on to it. Go through the opposition; don't get stuck in it and then allow your experience to define who you are. You are so much more than your core negative experiences. But it is by going through these experiences that you will discover that you are so much more.

What Do You Do with the Disharmonies and Misconceptions Once You Discover Them?

Once we discover these misconceptions, negative beliefs, and patterns, we are to let them go, which is exactly what this course teaches you. This is really why you are here, to learn what to do with them and how to move through them so that you may feel and experience joy. Each and every process taught in this course will assist you in moving through these patterns so that you may experience a joy-filled, happy life.

Is There More than One Way to Clear Your Disharmonies and Core Beliefs?

Yes, there are many techniques to help you release your core beliefs and negative feelings. I personally use every process taught in this book. Here is a brief list of the clearing tools that will be introduced in this course:

- Prayer
- Imagery
- Breath work
- The eight-step oneness process
- Rapid-eye technology

These are all great tools that will help you raise your vibration and move from your present state of being into an increased measure of joy.

16

Clearing Sessions: Why, When, and How

What Exactly Is Clearing Work?

Clearing work is the work of the divine; it is a very essential part of our existence. I believe clearing work is really the repentance process; it is about getting into the core of our beings, our hearts, and cleansing and purifying them.

We may think we know what is in our hearts, and to some extent we do. All truth that exists in the heart is there to stay. You have worked hard throughout your life to be the best you can be, to live a virtuous and honest existence. This is good, but this is not what I am talking about. I am talking about what is in your heart that you don't want in there. You see, we have many beliefs and perceptions within our hearts that are no longer serving us. They were put there in our early beginnings as formed misconceptions. Once these beliefs are formed, they remain in the heart until we become aware of them and choose to do something about them.

Tannie Bennett

Once you begin to understand this divine process, clearing out or purifying the heart can be a very easy, natural, everyday event.

You have been on earth for many years now, and you have a lot of "stuff" stored in your heart that is causing you grief. This is what clearing work is intended to remove. We do not want or have any intention of clearing out or changing the positive aspects of our nature. The positive areas of your life or your good works do not cause opposition. What causes opposition is anything in your heart that is not in line with your divine truth, anything that is not really in line with what you want to become.

Don't misunderstand me: our opposition and negative programming have their role and purpose. They were put there in the first place to teach and train us in becoming what we intended to become in our earliest beginnings. I believe they have done that. They have served their original purpose, which is why we are all about getting it out and letting it go now. Like replacing an old appliance, once you get a new one, there is no reason to keep the old one. But if you never knew how to get rid of the old, and in fact didn't even know if you should, I imagine your house would be pretty full of stuff that would simply get in your way. This is what our old patterns and perceptions are doing; they have served their original purpose by giving us the experience and the lessons, and now they are just getting in our way. They keep surfacing to remind us they are there. Once we recognize and notice them, we can then make another choice. We can choose to change them or simply let them go.

Do you know how to get rid of your old "stuff"—your old patterns, perceptions, and beliefs?

Most of us don't know how to or even understand that we should get rid of the old. Imagine your life if you had never gotten rid of anything since the day you were born. I believe things would be pretty crowded at your house. Well, this is the condition of your heart, or the core of your being; it is breaking down under the load of what is stored inside. It is time to clean it out. It is time to become pure in heart.

Our patterns and perceptions (the old stuff) surface in a very natural fashion. We never have to dig. Our job is to learn how to recognize when a pattern surfaces, what it looks and feels like, and then what to do.

I spent years digging and even took my clients digging. It was good; I learned a lot from the experience. I learned that it is much easier to just clear it as it surfaces. Imagine the work of digging for treasures. That would take a lot of time, expertise, expense, and energy. Now imagine if you knew that the treasure would surface, and all you had to do was recognize it when it came to the top. Think how much easier that would be.

Allowing our patterns to surface on their own is definitely the easier way. This is what I want to introduce to you now.

- How do you recognize a pattern when it has surfaced?
- What do you do to get rid of it?
- How can you be done with it once and for all?

All of our patterns are truly patterns, things that repeat themselves. What experiences have you had that keep repeating themselves? What do you keep doing over and over again? Is there a part of your life you want to change but you can't figure out how? (Refer to the practice exercise in Chapter 3, *Changing Your Life by Changing Your Thoughts.* You recorded there some of the patterns you discovered.)

Our patterns keep surfacing in an attempt to get our attention. This is what we want. We want all this stuff to surface. But if it doesn't catch our eye and we don't change it when it's on top, then it will surface again in a similar situation later on.

Think about your life for a moment. Do you have a routine when it comes to your finances or even discussions about your finances? Do you experience the same frustrations and situations over and over again? If so, you have a pattern there.

Do you have a problem with your children, your parents, or work associates that seems to never go away? If the answer is yes, you have a pattern.

You might say, "Well, I know I have some patterns running, but what is the next step? To me it all feels like frustration. Every time we talk about the subject, all I feel is anger and frustration."

Good, you have recognized the pattern. The next step is to get really clear about the feeling that this person or this situation is bringing to the surface. There may be many feelings that surface all at once—feelings of frustration, anger, rage, and annoyance. This is very typical; there is usually a lot of emotion attached to each pattern. The longer it has been ignored or avoided, the more emotion is attached to it. This is nature's way of getting your attention. You know, "the squeaky wheel gets the grease." The bigger it gets, the harder it is to ignore.

So we found a pattern, and it is loud and annoying. We have identified the feelings that this pattern has brought to the surface. What's next?

The best time to get rid of the pattern is when you are in the energy or the emotion of the pattern, when you are feeling the anger, annoyance, or frustration of the moment. Yet when you are "in" a pattern, when you are in the energy of the moment, most of the time you are so "in it" that you aren't thinking clearly and you just move on in the rage. This is what training is all about. We will begin practicing the clearing or release processes with the little patterns. As you practice the tools and are successful with the little ones, then when the really big ones come along, you will be ready to handle them. The more you practice, the easier it gets.

So here is how it works.

First, you discover your patterns or a problem, and then you wait until you experience a negative emotion. Believe me, you really don't have to wait long for that to happen. We experience negative emotion daily, especially when we are thinking about a problem. Thinking about them will bring the energy right up to the surface.

When you find yourself in negative emotion, you begin to use the tools that are taught in the course. The best tools, or the ones I use most frequently, are imagery, prayer and the eight-step oneness process which is taught in the following chapter. I figured a long time ago that God knew everything about me and that He would be the perfect one to help me out of what I was in. I was right; this worked for me so I kept turning to God for help. During my journey, I discovered many great tools that facilitated the clearing process. But, basically, what you really want to do is simply change. You want to let go of all the negative misconceptions and patterns in your heart and replace them with truth, love, light, and joy.

Once you discover a pattern and are in the heat of the emotion, you simply pray and ask God to help you release this pattern and change your heart so that you can become one with Him.

Get rid of the patterns or beliefs that keep getting in your way and cause significant opposition in your life. You don't need them anymore. Once you have had your experience with them and have gained the knowledge you set out to receive, you can then be complete with the process. It is like your school books. You don't keep them from year to year. You move on and get new ones and learn new things. You progress and have new experiences with new books that facilitate your growth and forward movement. You don't need to hold onto the old books once you have mastered them.

We are here to gain experience. Once we've had the experience that the misconception or negative belief has offered, we are free to move forward and have other experiences. We don't need to keep having the same ones over and over again. But as long as you keep the old stuff around, it is going to get in your way. You are going to experience the same patterns again and again until you are so sick of them that you turn to God in desperation and say, "Help! I want to change!" God, of course, is always listening, and as soon as you ask for help, it is on its way. My intention is to help you learn how to ask and what to look for when the answers show up. This too is a significant part of our journey to joy.

Throughout the course, you will learn how to let go of your old patterns while learning how to clearly communicate with God. It is a joyful process. You will love the results.

Once you have identified your pattern and are in the energy of the emotion, the next step is to simply pray and ask God to help you let this go. You can ask for that in a million ways.

Below are a few simple steps to help you release your old patterns and misconceptions. You will be clearing your memory storage tank, also known as your subconscious mind, your heart, or the core of your being.

Always remember to begin with deep, cleansing breaths. Deep breathing is the key that unlocks the doorway to your heart. Breath marks the beginning of life; it also marks the beginning of your new life.

After identifying the problem, get clarity on what you are feeling. When I catch myself feeling bad or not liking something in my life, I define it. Sometimes I use the "Because Tracks" to get clarity and gain more information about the feelings I am experiencing. This process is taught in Chapter 8 "Simple Techniques to Raise Your Vibration."

I then take the problem to God. I use these simple prayers:

Heavenly Father,
Would you please heal this memory, pattern, or perception experience totally and completely? Heal all the layers and levels of this experience and do everything that needs to be done to bring this pattern into complete resolution and healing. Then please restore my physical, mental, and emotional body to its original blueprint; restore it to what it was like before this pattern was placed in my experience.

Thank you,
In the name of Jesus Christ. Amen.

Sometimes, I simply say this:

Heavenly Father,
Would you please heal what I am feeling right now totally
and completely, bringing me and all parts of me back into my
original, whole, pure divine state?
Thank you, Heavenly Father,
In the name of Jesus Christ. Amen.

Sometimes I like to know the memories the patterns are connected to, so I ask for more information during my prayers. Understanding and restoring the memories they are attached to has helped me understand myself and others better. I feel I understand and know my parents and my early life situation better now than ever before. Having this insight has given me peace and clarity. It truly has been a gift of divine love.

Once you offer your simple prayer, your work is complete. It is then time to wait for the next episode of negative energy.

If we take care of our patterns or the negative energy as soon as they surface and let them go, we are really setting ourselves up for a great life. It is so freeing to never have to face that situation again. It is wonderful to be around family members and loved ones and not feel like you want to kill them, run away, or brace yourself for what is coming. I have loved feeling these changes in my life. You really do feel light and free, and it is so much easier to stay in joy when you don't have the weight and pull of your patterns hanging around your neck.

Sometimes, however, we will need help because of the energy or vibration of the stored pattern or belief. So for the really big ones—and sometimes they all feel big—I use imagery, the eight-step oneness process, or rapid-eye clearing sessions.

For more information about rapid eye, refer to the Rapid-Eye Technology section at the back of this book or go to the rapid eye website at http://www.rapideyetechnology.com. Once you have experienced what it feels like to "let go," then you can use the above simple processes with skill and confidence.

See how easy it can be? All it requires is a bit of time and experience. Remember that you can do anything you want and be really good at it. It is your destiny. You were born for greatness. Now how does that feel?

After Clearing Sessions, What Can You Expect?

We all have personal, family, and relationship patterns or issues we would like to change. These changes take place by getting to the core of the experience, allowing the mind and heart to connect and become one again (*heart* meaning the core of your being). Once this occurs, it is exciting to experience the new feelings and results. You have had moments of enlightenment or "ahah moments" in your past. This is the feeling that accompanies understanding and resolution.

"Happy is the man that findeth wisdom, and the man that getteth understanding. For the merchandise of it is better than the merchandise of silver, and the gain thereof than fine gold" (Prov. 3:13–14 KJV).

When we connect our minds and our hearts, when we "get understanding" about our own lives, we are most definitely on the road to joy and happiness.

After your clearing sessions, you will experience this exhilarating feeling and undergo very significant life changes. You will experience the same life situations but in a new energy, a new feeling, and with new, wonderful results. It is really quite exhilarating to experience these changes in your life when in the past you have tried so hard to change and nothing ever seemed to work.

This time around, life is going to be different. Watch for the subtle changes. Set your intention now to recognize and be aware of the positive results of your work because they will suddenly appear. All of a sudden, you will notice for a moment in time that your life is different and that you are no longer responding the same way. Even the people around you will behave differently. Believe me, this part gets pretty exciting and joyful.

Probably the most significant thing I experienced after my clearing sessions was an enormous sense of relief. When finished, I felt light and happy. I felt I could face another day. I loved improving my life, and I love living and being in joy.

After your clearing sessions, while the feelings and the results of your success are fresh on your mind, it would be a great time to record them in a positive emotion journal. Connecting to that divine part will be a very enriching, rewarding, joy-filled experience.

Not long ago, a friend who I hadn't seen for about eighteen months commented, "Tannie, you look great. You look like you have lost weight." I thought to myself, *Yeah, I have lost a ton (emotional weight). It is great that it is showing up on the outside.*

17

Getting Past the Heat of the Moment

Let's begin with many deep, cleansing breaths. When we begin each lesson with cleansing breaths, it will help you receive a deeper understanding of the material being presented. When the mind is fully oxygenated and the body relaxed, the mind can absorb the information on a fuller, more complete level. This is our intention for each lesson, each experience in this book. If you begin your work with deep, cleansing breaths, it will allow whatever you are working on to be more clearly understood and noticeably accomplished. Deep breathing is a simple yet powerfully effective technique to master.

Today we are going to discuss in greater detail the meaning and purpose of our opposition, dysfunctional patterns, and habits and how they serve us. We have discussed this throughout the course work to help you gain a more full and complete understanding of why life is the way it is and to help you understand and appreciate that your life's journey is really a perfect plan.

When you enter into a fully loaded opposition or trigger moment, like I did about thirty minutes ago, all of your frustrations, rage, and anxiety will rise full bloom to the surface. In that moment in time, you might feel ready to be done with your earth experience and eager to return to your heavenly home. Life has many such moments.

In the past, hitting something with such a power-packed charge of negative emotion would have wasted me for days. But today I am proud to admit that I had two huge "whopper" moments before noon. Yes, they were difficult. No, I did not understand the problems at the time. In fact, I wondered why I was going through them, what they were to teach me, and whether I could survive them alone. I wondered if I needed to call for help on these two problems. They were pretty intense.

So what did I do? I cried, I acknowledged my anger, and then I began to pray. But the real comfort came when I felt heavenly arms around me and felt the love I so often feel from my heavenly support team. Nothing was done other than what I am teaching you in this course. It was easy. My heavenly support team simply loved me. Then I asked for the help I needed, and it was done. I took some deep breaths, got up again, and began my day in a new energy while setting a new intention for the next segment of my day, in which I was to write this piece.

Each opposition experience will teach you something about yourself, something about life, and something about how much your heavenly support team is standing by, ready to assist you through those very difficult moments.

Today I learned *again* that love can heal anything, that asking for help from heaven is really the best way to get through the day, and that my heavenly support team is there just waiting to serve. I learned that letting go gets easier the more you do it. Even though we will always have opposition experiences and there will be times we'll feel bad, I learned that those experiences don't have to last any longer than it takes to pray about them and let them go.

In the situation that hit me today, I felt really out of control to do anything about the circumstances. It was a situation that needed immediate attention, so I did what I could and then let it go. Now I trust that it will all work out somehow, and the only thought I give to it is, that it is going to work out just as I want it to. I allow no other thoughts into my head, especially those that are contrary to the outcome I desire.

Even though I have been working this program for many years now, life continues. At times, significant challenges come my way—challenges so big that they stretch me a little further than the last one did. This is the purpose and intention of our opposition experiences. Each one is really a gift and a blessing. The key is learning to clear the energy of it so we can see the gift and the blessing.

These experiences are also intended to teach us that we are not alone and that someone really does care about what happens to us. In the past, we spent so much of our lives not knowing and not understanding that now, today, we feel we have to face our future the same way. We do not. We can have a new and different experience anytime we are ready. It is simply a matter of choice.

After the energy of this morning's moment was released and I expressed what I wanted instead, I let go and am now simply trusting God's will. I know it will all work out. And how do I know this? From my past experience of letting go and seeing it all work out.

You may wonder if you will ever get to the place of knowing things will work out and knowing you will make it through a huge trauma in a few minutes. But you will if you continue on. Becoming a master of anything takes practice and time. Becoming a joy master will take practice and time as well.

Let's see how fast you can turn yourself around from being in the heat of the moment to being in joy. Are you ready? Let's try one out with a new process called the eight-step oneness process.

Getting Past the Heat of the Moment

Practice

The Eight-Step Oneness Process

The eight-step oneness process is a wonderful clearing tool that is taught and practiced in the live Journey to Joy workshops, seminars, and courses. It is basically a working prayer. When you begin to use this process, it's easiest to work through it with a partner first and have him or her guide you through each step. Once you feel comfortable with it, you can easily take yourself through it with success and ease. If a partner is unavailable, simply set your intention to be successful at it and you'll do just fine.

The perfect time to work through this process is when you are in the heat of the moment or faced with a difficult life challenge.

When you are ready to try this out, refer to your workbook, where you will find an eight-step oneness process work sheet to assist you.

1. The Problem

The first step is to identify the problem you want to work on. Think of something that causes you stress or is really bugging you, or think of a significant life situation you are now facing. Do you have one in mind? Good. Write it down.

_____

_____

_____

_____

_____

_____

2. Your Feelings

Now, with this problem in mind, write down all of the feelings you experience because of this problem. These will be feelings that come to the surface when your thoughts are focused on the problem.

----

3. The Birth of the Problem

Next, let's discover the birth of the problem, or when you first experienced this situation in your life. Remember that when we connect to the birth of the problem, we can then easily bring it to resolution.

To discover the birth of the problem, you simply ask God in prayer to reveal this information to your mind. This information is stored in the subconscious mind, or in your cellular memory, and prayer is the quickest way to access that information. Once you ask God, He will bring the memory or a thought into your mind. Trust it. The memory will be of a time when you were very young, perhaps prebirth, at birth, or in early childhood, but generally it will be a memory before the age of eight.

Remember, we are programmed with our core beliefs at a very young age.

The memory that will come into your mind may also be a family experience. It may be a family pattern that has been in your family for generations. When this memory comes to mind, if you feel satisfied with the information you have received, you may continue on to the next step. If you don't feel satisfied, you will want to ask more questions until you feel content.

_____
_____
_____
_____
_____
_____

4. Understanding

Next, we are to ask God for more understanding of the problem. Once you have understanding, it is easy to move past your difficult experience and bring it to total resolution. Never move on before you reach understanding because understanding is "The Gold." This is why we had the problem or the experiences in the first place. We have these experiences so that we may learn and gain knowledge.

Once you feel satisfied and you understand why this problem was in your life and what you were to learn from it, you can then move on to the next step.

_____
_____
_____
_____
_____
_____

5. Pray to Remove the Problem

Step five is really easy. Here you simply pray and ask God to remove this problem, core belief, obstacle, memory, feeling, or stumbling block from your path. He can move any mountain, no matter the size. I use the following simple prayer for this step.

Heavenly Father,

Would you please heal what I am feeling right now, totally and completely, and bring me and all parts of me back into my original, whole, pure divine state, the state I was in before this pattern affected my experience?

Thank you, Heavenly Father,
In the name of Jesus Christ. Amen.

6. Ask for the Gift You Want Instead

Once God has removed the obstacles from your path, you will then decide what you want instead, which is usually the opposite of your problem. Knowing what you want is really easy at this point because you just experienced a big dose of what you don't want. When you have decided what you want to replace your problem or pattern with, you then ask God for that gift.

This is how He takes our weaknesses and turns them into our strengths, but it is important to understand that we have to ask Him first to take it and then ask Him to replace it with something better.

We need to ask for what we want in order to honor the law of agency. Agency is an eternal law. If you want any blessing from God, you have to ask for it. Imagine getting to heaven and saying to God, "Why did Susie get so many blessings and

I didn't?" God would simply answer, "Because Susie asked for those blessings." Can you then see yourself half-stunned, saying, "Oh"?

Once you ask Him to remove the problems and replace them with the opposite, you are almost done.

7. Results

The only thing left now is to watch for the new gifts to show up in your life. You will be watching for the results of your labor, and believe me, it won't take long for them to appear. You will in most instances experience an immediate change of heart, which will be very significant and satisfying.

When you become skilled in this eight-step process and in your communications with God, you can ask Him, "What is the outcome I can expect to see as a result of letting this problem go?" This is where the joy comes in. When you see a vision or a thought of significant change or wonderful gifts come into your mind, life can be pretty joyful.

8. Completing the Process

The last step is to ask God if there is anything you need to do to make this process complete. Sometimes there is action required, like forgiveness, or there may be movement of some kind, but God will tell you or you will feel what that action step is, if there is one. Once you finish this step, the process is complete—at least until you discover another problem or feel yourself in negative emotion and want to go through the process again.

Once you have run through this process several times, it gets easier. You can go through a huge trigger in as little as two to five minutes. Please give yourself practice time to get to that stage.

Review
Eight-Step Oneness Process

1. Identify the problem you want to change.
2. Identify the emotions this situation brings to the surface.
3. Connect to the birth of the problem by asking God to help you find it.
4. Gain understanding from God about this problem. This is the reason you had the problem in the first place. This is the knowledge you wanted to receive from this experience.
5. Ask God in prayer to remove your stumbling block or the cause of the problem. (Say the clearing prayer found in the book or use your own.)
6. Get very clear about what you want instead and then ask God for that gift.
7. Watch for the results of your change of heart, or ask God to show you what you can now expect to experience in life with this problem resolved.
8. Then the final step is to ask God, "Is there anything else I need to do to make this process complete?" Once you are finished, you will feel at peace and experience a wonderful, balanced state of being.

See how easy change can be? These steps are pretty simple. Once you begin this eight-step process of change, you will have a desire to continue on the journey because it will bring you such peace and joy.

Take time to practice this process daily, and you will have some amazing experiences. But most significantly, you will love the peace it will bring into your life.

Team up with a buddy and take him or her through the process. This too will be a joy-filled experience, and you will learn so much from your gift of service. It is easiest at first to work with a buddy and have him or her direct each step, and then all you have to do is receive the inspiration as it comes in.

This eight-step process is thoroughly taught in the live Journey to Joy courses and seminars. When you use this process daily, you will truly be on the road to joy.

18

Keeping an Emotion Journal

Recording your negative thoughts and emotional feelings daily will give you important information as to some of the prerecorded negative thoughts, patterns, and perceptions you have running. Often, these are family patterns and are so familiar that we are unaware of them. Recording them consistently will give you personal insight and valuable information.

You will not be able to change your life until you become very clear about what you want to change. If you have strong emotional feelings surface, begin your clearing process by recording them in an emotion journal or in the feeling section on your eight-step process work sheets. These emotions are important keys to your core patterns. They will also be a record of your success.

I once compiled the negative word patterns of my sisters and myself from our sessions and the conversations I had with them on the phone. The end product was a "family emotional script." It was a remarkable experience when I put them all together and read the script. It was as if I was rereading my childhood in the negative. The whole family was there: Mom, Dad, Grandma, and Grandpa. I could hear each of them in the words we spoke. This gave me very valuable information for my release work.

Below is an example of a negative emotion journal or script written by a client (used with permission) in preparation for her next session.

I'm SO sad ... so, so sad, want to cry.
Depressed.
Heavy.
Life sucks. What am I doing?
Can't make it, don't want to make it.
Hate my life, hate my job.
Can't get up to go to work, don't want to get up.
Don't want to go to work, or go to church, or grocery shopping.
Can't leave the house.
Want to stay in bed ALL day.
Don't want to leave the house, can't leave the house.
WANT TO GO HOME.
I made a mistake.
Can't get away, nowhere to go.
Can't go back, why can't I go back?
Depressed, angry, resentful.
Want to sleep, tired all the time.
Want peace, no peace.
Don't have a home, just want to go home, home is easy, home is fun.
GREAT discomfort, uncomfortable ALL the time.
No rest, no peace, tired, tired, tired.
Can't live like this, this isn't what I want. What am I doing?
Longing, missing, can it get any worse? Can I get any more unhappy?
Miserable, miserable with my surroundings.
This whole existence is stupid, and this isn't what I want.
I don't want this life.

I want a fun life; I want a single life, married life sucks.
There's got to be something better, can't go on like this.

This exercise helped her prepare for a session with me, but the same exercise could be used to prepare for clearing with the eight-step oneness process, imagery, breath work, or prayer.

19

Answering a Few Important Questions

Why Are Feelings Important?

One of the main reasons you came to earth was to feel, meaning to feel feelings in the physical body. Having a physical body is quite different from having a spirit body. There are similarities, but there are also many differences. Having a physical body makes the experience of feeling more complete. This very experience of being here on earth is an experience in feeling.

Once this plan of physical experience was set in motion, a whole new world was opened to us. In the beginning, before leaving our heavenly home, there were feelings of apprehension; gaining a physical body was going to be a totally new experience, one that had a lot of weight and merit as to our eternal progression. Our time on earth was to be relatively short, and there was much to accomplish while in this physical realm. Contracts were made, and paths were chosen. A lot of preparation took place before our spirits left the heavens to come to earth. Once the time arrived, it was similar to leaving home for the first time to go off to college. The anticipation and energy were high. There were many strong feelings, and these were permitted to remain with us for our earth experience, as you will understand and feel once you begin your clearing work. This simply adds to the experience.

As the spirits leave the heavens, they travel through the veil of forgetfulness. This wipes the memory of their heavenly home away so that their experiences on earth will be based solely on their time here. If everyone retained a remembrance of their truth, no one would want to stay because this experience is very different from our previous life in the heavens. The veil of forgetfulness is part of the plan. Remember that it is a perfect plan, and all elements of this eternal, perfect plan will be revealed in time.

The contrast of the experience of leaving the heavens and coming to earth is remarkable. Some have called it a real shocker, which indeed it was. Having a physical body is very different from having only a spiritual body.

In the beginning of our lives here, we make many judgments about the experience. If the judgments we make are in line with truth, then they will not cause or increase our individual opposition. If the judgments are out of alignment with truth (misconceptions), then they will enhance our experience in opposition. The lower the vibration of the judgment, the greater the opposition it will cause. Imagine believing "I am no good and unimportant" as opposed to "I am wanted and people are so excited that I am here!" The difference in these two belief systems would create a totally different life experience for the individual.

Judgment is the determining factor. When judgment is withheld, you are able to remain out of the opposition cycle. You are able to be in the world but not of it. *Judgment is the element that keeps you in opposition patterns or cycles.*

If at any time during the early birth or life experience, one makes this type of judgment or misconception, his or her opposition is set. Heavenly Father, in His wisdom, provides unlimited opportunities for us to see our misconception. This is why He has sent parents, teachers, and leaders to the earth. Look at your experiences alone. What have your parents or leaders taught you about love?

We are taught in our earliest beginnings that we are to love ourselves, love and honor our parents, and love one another. We are even taught to love our enemies and that love is the greatest commandment. Love surpasses all understanding. Love fulfills all the laws, and those who have this quality of love can comprehend all things. Love is very important to your earthly experience, but in order to really understand love, we begin by getting a taste of its opposite. Misconceptions at this early state are the perfect way to experience opposition.

This earthly life is not only a time to experience opposition but also a journey in remembering the love that we are. Our journey is about returning to the vibration from which we have come with all the knowledge and experiences of our earthly existence. It is not about losing anything; it is about gaining more, becoming more of who you really are. You can see from each of your experiences so far that you have gained valuable wisdom and experience. By the time you're finished with each experience, you are very grateful for the lessons learned because somehow this experience has added more to who you are. You have gained wisdom and understanding, and your eyes are opened. Each opportunity in opposition is intended to be a great gift. When you get the lessons and step into gratitude, you have passed the course and are ready for the next one. The course work gets easier as you are able to quickly step into gratitude because you have found joy in the experience.

Won't We Always Have Opposition while We Are Here?

There will be elements of opposition all around you. If you allow the elements to be as they are, withholding any judgment, you will not draw opposition to you. In each situation, you are looking for the perfection of the experience. Look for the lessons learned while choosing to stay out of judgment, knowing that it is all perfect. If we stay out of judgment, we are able to stay in joy. It is that simple.

We are told in the scriptures to "judge not." Judgment is what activates your magnetic pull. You see, each person is here to learn, grow, make choices, and experience opposition, and they are doing a fine job of it. So what part of the experience would you want to change for them? They are perfect, doing just what they came to do. Each person is learning, growing, and changing in his or her time frame, just as you are in yours. Remember that the only person you can choose for is yourself. It really is a perfect plan. The key is learning how to live the perfect plan, understanding how it is perfect, and how to respond so we can make the time here divine.

What Is the Purpose of Our Feelings?

Your feelings are simply your guidance system giving constant feedback as to how you are doing at becoming your best self and how you are doing in your earthly school of opposition. If you remain in touch with this guidance system and heed its warnings, your vibration will rise and then more of your DNA and life force energy will be activated. There are parts of you encoded to open and activate when a certain light level is reached.

Every bit of this earthly experience is important, both the negative and the positive. The negative life experiences you have are the fuel that rockets you forward into growth and eventually into joy.

It is better to pass through opposition than to get stuck in it. Getting stuck in opposition is like getting a recording stuck; it gets really bothersome. You listen to a song to enjoy it in its completion, not just hear a few notes over and over again. When we get stuck in a pattern or belief system, we are not experiencing the gift in completion. We are just hearing the same line over and over again. No wonder we're stressed!

After Beginning This Program, I Felt Really Agitated. Is That Normal? What Is Happening to Me?

When you begin working through this program, you will become more consciously aware of your negative emotions, stress, and agitations. As the negative emotions surface, do not become alarmed. This is what we are going for. We want the agitation and negative emotions to surface so we can let them go and bring the patterns or beliefs to resolution. It is this negative charge that you are carrying around that is causing your stress and contributing to the negative experiences you are having in your life. When you access this, you will have just hit gold. Celebrate the experience! It is coming out. If you get it out, you will be free. It will no longer have any pull to keep you in bondage to it. You will be free, free, free! This alone is a very joy-filled experience.

When I began, I did not have this perspective. I did not look at the uncomfortable memories and emotions that surfaced as a gift, but as I progressed I began to realize what an incredible gift this was. If you are never aware of what is keeping you stuck and in turmoil, then you are not empowered to change it.

When you become conscious of a part of your life that is out of harmony, then and only then can you change it. When you become aware of a disharmony in your personal life's purpose and goals, it will feel very uncomfortable; it will surface in the form of a negative emotion. This is not to say you are doing anything wrong; this is to say, "Here, you have just hit upon something in your life that is out of balance." Then, when you release the feelings, perceptions, patterns, and beliefs with the tools learned in the course and reframe the experience with what you want instead, restoring yourself to your original blueprint, you will then come into balance and alignment with your life's purpose and goals. You will then be able to journey on in joy and finally experience what you have longed to experience.

This is a process and it will take time, but the results are extremely significant. If you sincerely try—keeping a strong, focused intention—you will receive the encouragement you need to keep on the path.

In reference to negative emotions surfacing, I often ask my clients this revealing question: "When you squeeze an orange, what comes out?" The answer of course is obvious; it's orange juice.

Then I ask, "When you get squeezed or put under pressure, what comes out?" Think about that for a moment.

If it wasn't in there, it wouldn't come out. So if your life situations bring out the worst in you, it is really a good thing because then you are empowered to let it go and choose again. You have another opportunity to really get what you want and become the person you have always wanted to become.

I love working these principles, and I love working with the energy workers who have worked these principles for some time because they really understand that getting triggered is a good thing. When I call them to help me through a loaded trigger moment, they shout, "Yeah! Let's go for the gold!" Here I am feeling like "Grrrrrr," and they are happy for me because they know I am on a treasure hunt for knowledge, wisdom, and freedom and that soon I will feel light and happy and won't ever have to go through that experience again. So you see, even being triggered can become a joyful process.

What Causes Us to Be Out of Harmony with Our Life's Purpose?

Our internal guidance system is not being recognized and heeded.

From our earliest beginnings, we were gifted with this precious guidance system from our Father in Heaven, yet most of us were not taught how to use it effectively. This internal guidance system is an incredible system, and once you attune yourself to it, you will be able to move into your life's purpose with skill, joy, and ease.

The guidance system that we all have within us is a light sensor; it reads the vibrations of our thoughts. When we think a thought that is not in vibrational harmony with our original blueprint or our life's purpose and goals, then our divine guidance system will give us a warning in the form of a negative emotion. Most of us have not been taught that our emotions are our guidance system at work. We have been taught to bury our negative emotions, to buck up, and to grin and bear it. This is not how this system was intended to operate. The system is an informational system that will inform you, thought by thought, if you are in or out of harmony with what you want or with your life's divine purpose.

When we become very intentional about our health, relationships, and life and focus on what we really want with regard to them, then there is really nothing that can stand in the way of our joy and success, except perhaps ignorance.

If you really believe you are a child of God and that God is the father of your spirit, then you won't be satisfied with anything less than living up to your divine potential. You are a very significant and important person. You are the child of a deity. That makes you and your life here very significant! It is now time to step into your power and see yourself as God sees you. God knows who you are, and your internal guidance system is also well informed. Now it is time to get your life in harmony with your divine purpose and joyfully move into it. You will never be able to see your worth and your great purpose if you are spending your days fighting negative emotions and fighting your internal guidance system.

It is time to learn what to do with negative emotions. It is time to realize that these emotions are an incredible gift from God. Use them to lift you up instead of letting them weigh you down. It is time to rejoice and live in joy! We have lived in struggle long enough. Wake up to your great purpose and to who you really are. It is time to remove the veil of forgetfulness, come into your wholeness, and become one with God in purpose and deed. It is time for you to really see who you are and to heal from all the opposition you have faced in your life. It's time to cleanse your inner vessel, to clear all that is keeping you out of harmony with your divine purpose, and to let go of everything that is in the way of becoming the magnificent person you are.

What Causes Our "Stuff" to Rise to the Surface?

When you focus on certain events or people in your life you activate vibrational frequencies. If these thoughts or the object of your focus is in line with your divine nature and your personal purpose they will not cause opposition; you will not feel negative emotions from these thoughts. If they are not in line with your divine truth, you will feel the vibration of your focused thoughts. Your internal guidance system will send you the warning or the vibration of these thoughts. The lower the vibration of that thought or life situation the worse it will feel. If the vibration is negative, you then have the opportunity, in that moment, to change your focus and your thoughts to something that feels better. Once you change your thought channel you will feel the vibration of your altered thoughts which will cause you to feel good. Sometimes however when you lower your vibration through thought or focus, it will activate (trigger) lower frequencies in your personal belief system or DNA pool. If this occurs these feelings will surface and then changing your thoughts will be difficult because you have a belief or pattern there that is in need of resolution. If that happens, you will need to discover your core belief in order to change how you feel. If you are having a difficult time shifting out of negative feelings by changing your thoughts, it is most likely because you have activated a belief that is in need of resolution. If you take care of yourself quickly and rid yourself of the negative core belief you will never be triggered by that thought again, it will leave your life for good. If you ignore the feeling it may go away in time, but the next time you are in the same situation or focus on the same thoughts it will cause you to feel the same feelings. If you are ready to live and be in joy you will need to keep your focus on things that bring you joy and bring your negative core beliefs into resolution.

Is It Important to Complete the Imagery? Because Sometimes I Get Interrupted and Sometimes I Fall Asleep.

Every Journey to Joy course imagery is safe. The purpose in doing these imageries is to facilitate our movement into joy. It is not like a rapid-eye session, where completing the process is very important. Imagery is simply a tool to help you get at a very deep level the principles and information that will facilitate living and being in joy. It is a process to help you develop spiritual sight.

If your imagery session is a release session and you have fallen asleep, merely pick up where you left off and complete the experience. If you do not have the time, simply state, "My intention is to release everything I have worked on thus far and to receive the full benefits of my efforts." Intention is a powerful process; use it to make your life easier.

What Is the Purpose of Doing Imageries Every Day?

By participating in daily imageries, you are doing many things for yourself. You are establishing a pattern of hope.

When you spend time clearing out what you don't want in your life, you have room for what you do want.

It is a significant process. One purpose in doing them is to help you release your roadblocks, the things that keep hitting you in the face and getting in the way of achieving your goals.

Another significant purpose is to create what you do want. When you spend time in the imagery process, imagining what you want in great detail, you are in the creative process. Your powerful mind is actually organizing unorganized matter. This is why this process is so important. If you spend time organizing the elements to be how you want them in your physical experience, you are giving order to your life. You are creating a template for the elements to form around, thus creating the life of your dreams.

Do You Have to Create the Same Picture Every Day for the Creation to Manifest?

No. If you can spend focused time on a creation, get really clear about how you want it to be, and then allow yourself to get into the feeling of the creation, it is on its way. Your only job is to maintain the vibration of the creation. If while in the creation process you find yourself getting really happy and joy filled, this is the vibration of that creation. If you can maintain that vibration, you will be in alignment for the manifestation of it.

A word of caution, though: maintaining your vibration is a journey. This is something we will practice daily. So if you cannot maintain that creation vibration, don't beat yourself up. Simply know that allowing your vibration to dip will merely slow things down a bit, but that is okay too because you will learn so much from the process.

This is one of the reasons we are doing clearing work. All of your negative perceptions, beliefs, and patterns were created in a very low vibration. This is what contributes to depression and anxiety. You are in a low (depressed) vibrational state.

When you let go of those lower vibrations, you are able to raise yourself up to a higher vibration. Then in time you will be able to stay in the high vibration of your creation, and it will manifest because you will be on the same channel or frequency of the creation. And you will see it come forth.

So If I Don't See My Creation Manifesting, Have I Missed It?

No. It merely means you have a bit of work to do. It will show up in time. Simply trust the process.

Why Does It Take So Long for Some Things to Manifest?

There are many contributing elements involved, and it is difficult to say unequivocally what elements are involved in your particular situation. Commonly, the most significant contributing factor is maintaining that vibration. As you participate in this program, you will learn day in and day out how to stay in joy. When you are able to stay in that high joy frequency, you will be in a better position to see your creations manifest more quickly.

It is really the process of building your faith and maintaining the level of faith needed to see what you want manifest. We have a lot of fear in our hearts, which will cancel our efforts to walk by faith. Once you start to clear your patterns of fear, you will be able to maintain the level of faith and hope needed to experience your miracle.

Part III

Using the Course Material

20

Introduction to the Course

Journey to Joy is designed to bring you from your present state of being into increased and lasting joy.

The journey to joy is a process, a journey. It will take time. It is important to remember, though, that everything you learn along the way to this joy-filled state is very important—every bit of knowledge and every experience. Do not allow your thoughts to go into the negative zone because of your expectations. The rule of thumb for the journey is this: "If you could do it any faster or any better you would. Therefore, your progress is just perfect." Always remember this as we travel together.

This course is designed to be a work you actively participate in. It is designed to be used on a daily basis.

A significant element to remember is the importance of deep breathing in the learning process. Within the framework of the course you will have time to meditate and experience what you are learning. Deep breathing during this time will help cement that information to a deeper level.

The course uses imagery to teach you new ways of doing things and a new way of thinking. Imagery is one of the tools used to reprogram your brain computer and rewrite your life script. If you will take thirty minutes a day with this work, it will change your life. There are many effective healing tools included; some you may be familiar with and some may be new to you. All are very effective if used faithfully.

This is a work in a work, meaning you can use this course work over and over again. Each time you use it, you will gain new insights and have new and different experiences because you will be different each time you experience it. You will be growing, changing, and increasing in knowledge and experience, so I would encourage you to use the course material again and again.

The imageries will take you through a great process of growth. You will be asked to experience and do things that quite possibly you have never thought of or done before. It is from this process—doing things differently—that you will gain your greatest growth. At times you will be asked to do things for which you may not understand the purpose, but if you'll trust the process and experiment, you will find the results of your efforts and this process to be truly amazing.

Most of us walk through life never thinking things through because we are so busy responding to the stimulus of our outside world. Very few of us ever take the time to go inside and get an "inner view." This work is about taking time out of our busy lives to go inside and discover what is in our hearts.

You are truly amazing, but because you have believed and accepted your negative experiences as your truth, you are not seeing your real truth. It is time to stop. It is time to stop and take time out of your busy life to go on an internal vacation. This will be a time to rest, a time of renewal, a time to ponder and meditate. It will be a time to find answers to some very significant questions about your life, such as the following:

- Who am I?
- Why am I here?
- What is my life all about?
- Why does my life feel the way it does?
- What is my specific purpose here on the planet?

- How do I change my life to have more peace and joy?

Have you ever wondered about any of these questions?

Perhaps you have felt like this: "I feel things inside, like somehow there is so much more to me, yet I don't know how to access that part of me."

Or perhaps you have thought, "I long for greatness, but I sometimes feel I can just barely get out of bed. Unless greatness falls in bed with me, it is not going to be mine."

Let me tell you a wonderful little secret. Greatness is in bed with you! It is lying just inside your skin, and together we'll learn how to get it out of bed, turn it on, and discover the magic, power, and true greatness that lie within.

Are you ready?

Are you ready to turn your life around?

Are you ready to stop struggling and fighting life?

Are you ready to learn to get into the flow and begin to experience joy?

I sure was! This is why I have received what I have received. I stopped dead in my tracks one day and prayed my little heart out, asking to be shown another way. And guess what? I got it! And here it is in a step-by-step process. It took time to stop the struggle patterns because that was how I approached every aspect of my life. But as I persisted on my journey, my life really began to change course. I really think I turned 180 degrees that first year. Since then, life just keeps getting better.

21
Journey to Joy

Course Overview

- Read the Journey to Joy course manual and become familiar with its contents.
- Complete the practice sheets found at the end of each lesson. A larger version of the practice sheets and more examples have been included in the student workbook.
- Start each day with intention, meditation, prayer, and deep breathing. Become intentional about the way you feel; become intentional about living and being in joy.
- Practice daily the clearing and release processes that are taught in the book, in the Journey to Joy seminars, and in the courses.
- Write your course intention—the road map for your journey and the road map to your success.
- Use the imageries daily. Taking time out for you is the only way to live and be in joy. Taking personal time out is true evidence of self-love.

- Share something you have learned with a friend. You both will be blessed.
- Experience the affirmations, stories, and the recorded imageries and practice the tools taught throughout the course.
- Keep your eye on the end results. Focus on the outcome, not the growth.

After the course is complete, I would encourage you to continue to use the tools and material. Create another intention, another roadmap, and begin a new marvelous journey to joy. Remember to stay connected to your new support team; this will help you stay on the road to joy!

22
Testimonials

Read what previous course members had to say about their Journey to Joy experiences.

"The first couple of nights during this class, I looked around the room and saw ordinary men and women. I saw people that struggle with the daily demands of raising children, maintaining relationships with their spouses and extended family, finances, and generally not knowing which way life was leading them.

"As this class has unfolded, I've watched each one of these men and women blossom. They are now what I would call extraordinary. Their faces are glowing, and I hear changes in the words they use. I have watched them transform before my eyes. They no longer struggle with daily life; they now see each challenge as a chance to learn something and to better themselves. They are hopeful, exuberant, positive, and really, truly happy. I've watched them explore and discover their lives' purposes, embrace them, and move forward toward them. The best part of all of this is the process; it has been done so fast, easy, and with grace. There has been no concentrating to make sure they remember the right way to say things or think about things. It just is.

"It has been a life-changing experience! It has been an awakening of my inner self. I am now seeing my true self, not being blinded by the false self. I now remember that we are all perfect. We are after all children of God; we are made in His image and He is perfect."

Lora D.

"It's a miracle! Thank you, thank you, thank you! I can't believe the change. I still have lots to work on, but I'm seeing improvements. Thanks again for this wonderful program."

Jana B.

"The course is awesome! I have learned so much about myself. I feel like I have hope in my life now. I can actually look past today. I have found out what I am going to be doing in my life! I feel lighter and happier. Tannie, I am so thankful for what you went through, and that you chose to share it with us; it has been such a blessing in my life. I won't ever be able to tell you what this has meant to me, because it is such a wonderful blessing to my life. I now love life."

Bobby H.

"I have so enjoyed letting go of the junk, and learning it is not all me, that some of it is DNA. I have enjoyed finding out why I have made certain decisions in my life, while getting to know myself better and learning what makes me tick. I now have tools to help me to de-stress and to change out of old negative blocks so I can have more peace in my life. I want to continue learning and make what I have learned a larger part of my life. I am thankful for Tannie and her gifts of healing. That foundation of how the Savior heals is apparent to me by these teachings. Thank you, Tannie. I love you."

Carla B.

"Taking the course truly was a joy! All the techniques have helped me so much. But I think what really inspired and helped me the most was our class nights. Being amongst the other class members and seeing them change, and seeing their joy, helped me to keep focused on my personal goals. I have learned so much; each part was so uplifting and helped me to always want to be in this high vibration of joy."

Ann J.

"Tannie Bennett took me on a journey that has forever changed my life. I am amazed at the things that I learned about myself. I discovered why I think the way I do and why I react the way I do. Life has become joyful and fun, and I am discovering new things about myself on a daily basis. I face each day with new courage. I laugh more, love more, and enjoy my family more than ever. This journey cleansed my soul and left me yearning to learn more, to reach new heights and expand myself. I don't doubt myself anymore. I see myself in a whole new light. I look forward to continuing my Journey to Joy so that I can keep discovering new and wonderful things about my life. The biggest thing I noticed from the class is the change in my family. I am so thankful for the opportunity to have taken the course. I look forward to more opportunities to grow and learn and move forward. I am excited to see change and to move into a higher vibration and stay there. Thanks."

Sandy L.

"Tannie took me on a journey of self-discovery, healing, and new beginnings. She helped me discover my true self and my divinity, which I had forgotten because of the fear and anger I let dominate my life. I am so thankful for the tools she gave me to help me always stay on my 'high' and to help me dance, laugh, and breathe each day. All I can say is I love the journey and experience and look forward to continuing the joyful journey. Thank you, Tannie, for blessing my life with the miracle of the class. I am eternally grateful."

Debi B.

"It was so wonderful! It was so good! It is so nice to have joy back in my life and to have it so much bigger and better than I had before. I am now looking forward to a brighter future. I am looking forward to more joy.

"Life from here on can only get better. I have loved learning to trust myself and know that I can get my own answers so quickly, and know that I am getting the right answers. I have loved seeing the change in me and my family.

"Time after time when I didn't feel good or when I was sick, after doing the imageries I felt better and I was ready to go again. It's a great tool. My session experiences were so great. I am getting clear and feeling and seeing more light and more and more joy in my life. I have been able to more clearly discern the spirit, and those experiences are becoming more frequent and stronger. But the part of the course that inspired me the most and facilitated my movement into joy was gratitude. To feel so much joy from focusing on all my many blessings and feeling the great joy high more often was wonderful. To feel my Heavenly Father's love through gratitude is wonderful! Tannie, you are a great teacher. Thanks."

Rene B.

"Overall it has been great! I have loved each lesson. The sessions are the best. The curriculum is good stuff, and I am very glad to have the imagery CDs. I am excited to share what I have learned with others, and at the same time I need to really work it and learn it for myself. I personally feel I need more emphasis on using and working the tools. Most important, I am in Joy!"

Beth P.

"I would recommend the *Journey to Joy* course to anyone. I felt I was a pretty normal person without any need of therapy. I wasn't sad or depressed. But in truth I wasn't really joyful either. I felt that life was a test to be endured, and part of the test was to remain cheerful. But joyful, really joyful? I didn't think it was possible.

"Some of the things I learned from the course include:

- It is possible to have joy in this life under any and all circumstances.
- It is possible to change your mood in an instant.
- There are techniques that can be used by anyone and everyone to calm their troubled soul.
- Everyone can benefit from sessions.
- Our intentions mold our life experiences.
- There is a good reason for us being 'triggered.' It is so that we can identify the areas that we need to address in our life. Are others not triggered in the same circumstance? Why are we? Can we do something about that?
- I learned to use the word 'because' to find out what is the root of our problem and then give the root cause over to the Savior so He can carry that burden.

"Because of this course I have come to a point where I experience a degree of joy most of the time. When I do have down times, I know what to do to change it all around."

Lois W.

"My journey started out on a really rough path full of stress, discouragement, anger, depression, etcetera. Through this course I have learned the tools to live a healthy, joyful, fulfilled life. My sessions were amazing, and I am starting to be able to get things on my own. It is amazing. I loved the people that were in the class and feel so supported in my journey. It is the start of having a more amazing, abundant, happy life."

Cherisse B.

"I have been able to understand more about myself as I have continued in this course. I am glad to have learned different methods to help identify and understand the negative feelings that are in my life and to learn ways to help release the low vibrations as they come up. My goal has changed; I will now search for the higher energy vibrations and try to minimize the lower ones. Thanks for helping me see the Joy in the Journey."

Michelle B.

"Every part of the course was great! Every part fit together in a very synergistic way. I have learned so much and it's been such a 'hands on experience.'

"My session experiences were very helpful in both teaching me and helping me clear negative beliefs. Learning through the imageries has been outstanding. I intend to continue using them every evening. They help me sleep better and help me have a more positive outlook when I wake up.

"Tannie is a great teacher because she teaches from experience and from her heart."

Judy B.

"I have grown so abundantly. I am so grateful that I discovered this course. I have changed and become more confident in my own power and in my divinity. I have cleared so many of my family and DNA patterns, and I feel so free. I have loved Tannie's stories; they are so full of lessons to learn. I would say they are similar to Christ's parables—a nice story with deeper meaning hidden in the story. I look forward to continuing my journey to joy. Because of my course experience, I was able to get a new home."

Cindy P.

"I loved the *Journey to Joy* course. This is my second time taking it, and I feel I have learned so much more this second time around. Class is great! It is so much fun being there with everyone and having experiences with them. I enjoy participating and also learning from other questions and points of views. I really enjoyed reading through the manual. Tannie presented the information in a way that was easily understood and easy to take in. I loved doing the sessions and clearing my issues and seeing how those sessions affected my life. I am so grateful for the opportunity to grow and to take this class again."

Christie J.

Anonymous Comments from Previous Course Members about the Course

"I loved it! It was very helpful."

"I believe that with these tools and techniques I can start managing my life for the first time, believing that I am in control and have the power to choose to live my life the way I want it to be."

"I have enjoyed the course; it has helped me think and find things that were blocking my progression. It is a wonderful thing."

"There were a lot of beautiful and wonderful truths taught and shared."

"The course is great; I am learning so much."

"It was wonderful. I loved it. It really helps me focus on good and happy feelings. Tannie is such a great teacher."

"I enjoyed the course; it was a great lesson in how to put into practice 'seek and ye shall find.' It is also a good lesson in taking time for your own healing, knowing that you cannot help others until you take the time to heal and learn."

What Clients Have Said about Their Session Experiences

"I have been in traditional therapy for seven years, and I have made more progress in three sessions with Tannie than all seven years put together. Thanks, Tannie, I love you."

Celeste Jones

"I have loved my sessions. I come in feeling crummy and leave feeling great. I feel like I would love one everyday! I wish everyone could feel the shift after six sessions and the hope it gives. I have learned so much about me and I have found more peace in my life."

Bobby H.

"My personal sessions with Tannie have all ended up being personal parables, like a mini video. The images that I walk through are simply orchestrated, and quite spontaneous, spiritual experiences. I simply hand over the monsters of my life, packaged in a neat bundle, like a rock, to a being of light and he takes them and turns them into light. My path is clear, and my reframe blossoms as a flower with a sweetness that fills the air. I then feel grounded, complete, and light, with joy in my heart. All this in about twenty minutes. I love this process."

Sylvia F.

"Thank you for validating my experience! I just want to get on with the work so that others can be healed as profoundly as I have been. Knowing that I have only begun this work and have only 'touched the tip of the iceberg' has made me anxious and excited to get moving. I want to continue with the feelings I have been experiencing, and I want it to touch every aspect of my life. I'm ready to be taught all the lessons I have to learn. I am willing, ready and able to follow the path that is laid before me.

"I don't think you really know how grateful I am for you. You have been a total blessing to me. I have been so inspired by you. You have helped me have the *courage to open my eyes. Thank you soooo much.*

Laura

"I think the thing I noticed almost immediately afterwards was I felt like I could breathe again. I didn't realize how much I wasn't breathing until I could. Since my session I have noticed lots of other things as well. The biggest change I think I have noticed is this new desire to do all those little things that I wanted to do in the past, but I felt I couldn't for one reason or another. Things as simple as taking the initiative in a conversation or project, and even going back to school, which is something I longed for, but for some reason I just felt I couldn't. I've noticed I'm a little more proactive with my life, rather than just sitting back and waiting for things to happen. It's like the fear and even apathy that kept me from accomplishing these things before is gone. I find that I am happier and a little more at peace with who I am. Not that my life is perfect now, but I feel good and I am content to keep trying and to better myself every day, whereas I wasn't before. Thanks so much for sharing your gift!"

Bethany S.

"A few years ago, my life changed for the better after having sessions with Tannie. I experienced tremendous relief from the stress of sexual abuse. Before this experience, my outlook on life was hopeless, and I thought that I was not to feel joy ever again. Wow, now after my sessions, I feel joy and hope. When problems occur in my life, I can deal with them without all of the *drama* and struggle that I used to experience.

"Tannie skillfully and gently provided a very comfortable and trusting environment for me to work in. With her skill and this winning technology, my sessions sailed by with light speed and ease. I am forever thankful for Tannie."

K. Satterwhite

"Having a session with Tannie is like taking a deep breath of fresh air. It is like stepping into a higher sphere. Her rare gifts and talents have helped me wipe the mud and grime off my windshield of life so I can see clearly to become my best self."

Tamara F.

"I love my sessions with Tannie. She has great intuition, and she follows it to help you in the best way possible. I call it 'cleaning house' because we really get to the nitty gritty and throw away the garbage. For example, I was given the homework to write my family script (negative things my family was saying). In my next session with Tannie, we worked on those sayings. My family has not said any of those things since, and they don't have a clue about what I was working on! It is amazing!

"In another session I wanted to work on feeling and expressing love better. I was amazed to get home and have my youngest child who is usually quite reserved open up and squeeze my neck with glee. She felt the change in me and has been so much more fun-loving ever since.

"This is leaps and bounds past the regular counseling or therapy. It is quick and right to the core. You can see results immediately. My family and I are becoming better and happier people. It is great!"

Beth P.

"My sessions with Tannie have literally changed my life. How? I'm not afraid of my life anymore. I don't have a college education (yet), and have depended completely on my husband. Now facing divorce I've gone from a scared, co-dependent, 'what am I going to do' state, to becoming completely independent, working my way through school, and having an amazing future in front of me. The biggest change is that I am not afraid, and I can take care of myself. Life has become a dream that I am continually enjoying because I'm learning to create it! Everything I've wanted I'm creating. Best of all, I'm doing it on my own terms and not through someone else! My future is so bright. When I first came to Tannie, I was panicky, scared, and emotionally exhausted. Tannie has assisted me in clearing the 'debris' that was keeping me from seeing who I really am. She has helped me discover her; she has helped me see my true self, and you know what I saw? Me, to like the tenth power, and I love her. I love being *me*! And there's nothing I cannot do. Thanks, Tannie!"

Lovinna

"Tannie, thank you! Thank you for listening and accepting the 'assignment' to bring this pathway of gentle yet powerful imaging to those desiring to walk the path to 'wholeness.' As I reflect back over the session we did on the phone I marvel at the awakening and new understanding I received as doors and walls were removed. I am so very grateful for the sense of peace and joy it has brought into my life! Thank you!"

Sally S.

"Tannie Bennett has such a gift; she is an amazing MRET. She has the ability to bless all those she comes in contact with. Just hearing her voice soothes my soul, uplifts me, and comforts me. She makes people feel like they can do anything. Her abilities are astounding, as she always holds everyone in unconditional love, and I always feel safe in her presence. Thanks, Tannie."

Brook

"With great apprehension and little understanding I entered Tannie's office as a favor to my mother. She had heard of the experience of a friend's daughter and thought a session might be helpful for me as I was working through some major life decisions and was seeking direction. I felt that if there were answers I needed for my life I should be on my knees asking my Heavenly Father for guidance instead of this. I was determined that if I felt uncomfortable with any portion of the session I would excuse myself.

"As I entered Tannie's office I felt a peace that encouraged me to stay and find out more. Through Rapid Eye Technology I was able to open doors in my mind that had long since been barred, helping me to understand where negative thoughts and impressions had been formed and how they continued to affect my choices, actions, and ultimately my life. I was able to see the positive relationships that uplift and encourage me to reach my potential. With clarity that only comes through the Holy Spirit I was able to understand my great and eternal worth. With healing that only comes through the atonement of Jesus Christ, I was able to remove from my thoughts negative feelings and impressions that were impeding my progression toward exaltation. I realized that the Lord was not being taken out of this healing equation. Instead I was being guided through the barriers in my physical being by one who understood better than I, to come unto Him.

"I continue to turn to the Lord daily for instruction and inspiration through the Holy Ghost but I am grateful for my experience with Tannie. I was so moved by the experience that I plan to work in the field eventually to help others in the same way I have been helped."

Stasha L.

"Tannie, I just want you to know how grateful I am for the work you have done with me. We have been doing sessions for quite some time now, and I have felt many shifts and gained great insights. However, our session yesterday confirmed without a doubt my testimony of the value of your work. I can't tell you just how amazing the change in my life that session has made. I was able to release so much of the pain, anxiety, guilt, remorse, and even despair that I have carried deep in my soul for over fifty years! Much of it wasn't even mine but what I had received from generations before me. I have not felt this kind of peace in many years; I didn't know it was possible. Today I find hope and an assurance that all is well, I'm on my right path ,and the desires of my heart will manifest. Everything will be all right. I look forward to our continued work together.

"You are one of my greatest gifts. I thank you and love you with all my heart."

Lewetta P.

Experiences with Tannie's Imageries

Shortly after I received this material, I was directed to produce a trial CD. I entitled it In Bloom. *I sent the CD out to many of my associates and friends all over the country to experience it and then report back their results. I believe those who used it as directed experienced the most profound results.*

Working with this CD and the imagery process has given me some of the sweetest experiences I have ever had in my life, experiences so sacred I have shared them with only a few. This is what awaits you as you diligently embark on your personal journey to joy and experience this amazing imagery process.

"I can't begin to tell you what listening to your CD has done for me, except WOW! The breathing and relaxation exercise in 'The Gift' was amazing; I felt calm, light and peaceful. I got very emotional as I was breathing and releasing the negative feelings I felt about my body. A year ago I had a C-section, which has left my once-140-pound body an undesirable 30 pounds more. But, after listening to these imageries, I know that if it were not for this body and what I went through I would not have my darling little boy. I felt so relaxed and peaceful. I saw myself skinnier and then when I looked into my Savior's eyes I knew it didn't matter anyway because nobody sees me that way, except me. I know my Savior loves me, as well as my husband and children. I can't wait to listen to the rest. I am so grateful to have been given the opportunity to hear this first part. You did an amazing job. Both the words and the music are life changing. It is perfect."

Jeannine

"I love the CD. I know it was divinely inspired. I learn something new almost every time I listen to it. I am grateful for the opportunity to heal from this beautiful imagery. Thank you so much."

Joyce Bailey

"I have really loved the imageries; they have opened up a whole new world."

Jo

"I loved your imagery CD. Experiencing the imageries has helped me view my life in a new way … a way that has been very healing. Thanks for sharing your gift with me."

Valerieann Giovanni
Artist, Author, MRET

"I love your guided imagery CD; I think it is impeccable. The gently flowing tones of your voice, like cool breezes, relax and refresh. Its powerful images moved me profoundly. I felt that I was being whisked on the wings of angels to another world where indeed I walked with Jesus, looked into his eyes, and was healed. I am not the same after having experienced it, and I find myself believing that, like Pinocchio after his encounter with the Blue Fairy, I am somehow more real because of your gift. Thank you for being who you are."

Cathy Bjerkan

"Thank you for this wonderful experience. In the beginning I questioned it, because I had a lot of release work going on. Now after continued use I can see what an amazing gift this has been to my life. It was named appropriately. I have been so blessed with the gift of this imagery. When I reached the point of doing it on my own, just going through the process I had some incredible spiritual experiences. It was so fun because a close friend was doing it with me and she had similar experiences. This inspired me to keep at it and then life became truly divine. Thank you so much for allowing me to be a part of this work; it has truly blessed my life."

Allie

"This is truly a work of divine love. I can feel the love that comes through each time I listen to it. 'The Gift' is my favorite imagery. I love to listen to that part when I see myself walking with the Savior, and I am healed by his touch over and over again.

"This CD makes me feel like it is truly that easy. All I need to do is breathe and have faith and unconditional love. I know one can heal by simply listening to this CD with the intention of healing. I now look at my body as a gift, and I am so grateful for that gift and all it does for me."

Stephanie F.

"The CD is fabulous. It helped me feel important as to who I am in my relationship with my Father in Heaven and feel the love that is meant for me. I am finding out what my commitments are that I made to Him in my pre-mortal state and fulfilling them while I am here on earth, being that special flower and blooming to my fullest capacity with his love and guidance. I am so excited to open those doors that haven't been opened yet and find out what is behind them. I am now in celebration of fulfilling my journey! Thank you so very much for giving of yourselves to create this wonderful gift for others."

Bonnie H.

"I never really looked at my body as a gift. I kind of thought of it as just another step on the way, a temptation, a hindrance, but it isn't. It is so beautiful and works so wonderfully for me.

"I can't even express in words what I saw or felt; it was just a deep, abiding joy. It was exactly what I wanted, that peace and joy. I feel like a better person with more light to share. I feel like every smile I give comes from my spirit and has the ability to touch another person. It was remembering music; I almost remembered more than was being said and played."

Amanda V.

"I just completed an experience of incredible endurance for me. I climbed Mt. Baldy. It took sixteen hours; the last two we walked in a downpour of freezing rain. I felt as if I could not put one foot in front of the other; I was consumed with exhaustion. I thought, *What is a fifty-four-year-old mother of ten who doesn't exercise often doing trying something like this?* I couldn't give up. My purpose in sharing this is because every muscle in my body was aching tonight, but something happened as I relaxed and listened to your imagery and music: the pain left me.

"Thank you so much for your gifts and intuition. I am so excited for the healing that can take place."

Shawna J.

23

My Course Intention

A Preview of Coming Attractions

Imagine looking into the future. (Choose an element of time you want to work with—eight weeks, six months, one year). What will your life be like at the end of the course if you experience the changes you desire? Record your expected results below. Get a very clear picture of what you want. This exercise is very important; you are creating your blueprint for change. What do you want?

Remember that we are focusing on the end results. What will your life look like in the future? Dream and record your thoughts as if your dreams were fulfilled.

Use this to get you started: "I am experiencing wonderful life changes as a result of my participation in this course. This is what my life is like now."

_____

_____

_____

_____

_____

_____

_____
_____
_____
_____
_____
_____
_____
_____
_____
_____
_____
_____
_____
_____
_____
_____
_____
_____
_____
_____
_____
_____
_____
_____
_____
_____
_____
_____
_____

Note: An intention worksheet has been included in your
workbook.

24

How to Use Journey to Joy Imageries

We have discussed the healing benefits of deep breathing and of using imageries on a daily basis. Now I would like to introduce the significance and importance of the imageries presented in this course and detail how to use them to get the best results.

You will find that the Journey to Joy course imageries are unlike any other imagery you have used in the past. These are intentionally interactive. In part they are to help you develop and improve your connection to your inner self and strengthen your connection to the divine while increasing your personal capacity to experience joy. These imageries are intended to be used on a daily basis.

Each imagery has a specific intention, which is written in each introduction. The imagery's intention is of course the goal or purpose for that imagery. It is also very important to state your own intention before you begin each imagery session to enhance the gift of the experience. As you do so, you will be declaring the benefits you are intending to receive from participating in that imagery. Your journey to joy is really all about what you want, so let's begin by stating it at the beginning of each imagery session. I will assist you in the beginning by making *personal intention suggestions* under the heading of each imagery title. The intention suggestions will be written below each imagery's intention. Remember, though, that these are only suggestions to help you get started. Feel free to set your own intentions when you are ready.

In the beginning your intention may simply be to experience the imagery and to learn what you can from it. Then, when you become familiar with the imagery and the process, you may set more specific intentions. We will continue to learn about setting intentions throughout the course through the written material and your personal experiences.

Adding your intention to the imagery's intention is a very powerful and important process. Do not underestimate the value of it.

The imageries in this beginning course are unique. They each have a specific intended goal or outcome. All of the imageries are interactive. In some you will be asked questions, in some you will be asked to imagine certain events, and in others you will be asked to retrieve memories of a past experience. Therefore, you will need time to tune in to your inner knowing, to get the answers or take part in the suggested experience.

If for some reason you are unable to do what the imagery suggests, do not be dismayed. You will have just discovered a roadblock. In the course, I will teach you how to remove your roadblocks so that you may journey on in joy. Once you have removed your roadblock, try the imagery again. You will be amazed at the totally different and wonderful experience you will have. (How to remove your roadblocks will be covered in Chapters 16 and 17.)

Many of the course members have used the imageries to help their spouses, friends, and loved ones through their difficult life situations. When you use them daily as suggested, they are easy to memorize. One of the most frequently used imageries in the course is the imagery "Letting Go." This is a simple release imagery. Once you become familiar with it, you may alter the imagery to fit your particular needs. For instance, one of the course members used it on her husband to help him through a particularly stress-filled day. Since dancing was not his forte, she changed the imagery to something he could relate to, which was golf. In the imagery, she created a bucket of multicolored golf balls. She instructed him to pick up a ball, identify the color and what it represented, and then hit the golf ball out into the distance and away. It was a great experience for them both.

You may also use the imagery "Letting Go" as a preventive tool by taking time each day to let go of anything that presents itself. All you need is time and a comfortable, quiet environment in which to experience the imagery.

As you gain experience with these imageries, they will begin to take on a life of their own. Trust this. You will be glad you did. For instance, during the imagery "Letting Go," you may experience a scarf that won't fly away. If this occurs, simply begin to ask questions. This will help you understand what is happening. We have not yet learned everything that some patterns are to teach us. Ask what else you need to know so that you can let this pattern go.

If you have a scarf that you instinctively want to keep, ask what it represents. They can also represent the positive or spiritual gifts that we are in need of. I personally have experienced this imagery where most of the scarves represented something positive. They represented something I was in need of at that time. Simply trust your inner knowing, and you will have a wonderful experience.

When to Use the Imageries

You may use the Journey to Joy imageries at any time and in any order during the course. Simply trust your personal guidance system as to which one you need today.

As you move through the course for the first time, you may have many questions. I would suggest that you write your questions down and continue to read because the answers to each of your questions will probably be found later in the course work. If the course work has not given you the answers you are seeking, don't worry. Within the framework of the course, I will teach you how to get answers to every question you may have.

The Emergence Process or Grounding Sequence

Once your imagery session is complete, it is important to become present and alert. You have been in a very relaxed state. Below are a few suggestions that will help you emerge to a fully awakened state.

Please use the emergence process at the end of every imagery session.

- Take in a few more deep, cleansing breaths with your eyes wide open.
- Drink a glass of cool water, eat a mint, or apply peppermint oil to the tip of your tongue or to your temples.
- Deeply breathe in the outside air.
- Walk barefoot through the grass.
- Move your body around.
- Press all of your fingertips firmly together.

Once you feel fully present and alert, you may check yourself by asking a question with numbers in it, such as "What year is it?" or "How old am I?" If you are in an altered state, you will not know the correct answer. If you realize you don't remember the year or date, simply say to yourself, "I am coming forward into the present moment; I am awake and alert." Then simply give yourself a bit more wake-up time and ask the question again. It should only take a minute more. If you are not fully emerged or grounded, you will feel spacey and unfocused. If you try to drive in this state, it will be easy to get lost.

Please do not worry about doing the imageries or the course wrong. An experience is never wrong; it is simply an experience. Each time you use the imageries, you will gain valuable information about yourself. You will become more comfortable with the practice of using imageries with each experience, and soon you will find your own way with them.

May you have wonderful imagery experiences.

An experience is never wrong; it is just an experience.

25

Journey to Joy Imageries:
Introductions and Intentions

Each imagery's introduction and purpose and a suggested personal intention have been included below the imagery's title. When you are ready to participate in an imagery, refer to the imagery's introduction and then choose and set your personal intention, place the imagery CD in your disc player, and begin.

At the end of the imagery experience, remember to use the emergence process to bring yourself back into an awakened and alert state. Recording your unique imagery experience may also be very rewarding. Refer to your Journey to Joy workbook for your imagery record sheets.

The Gift

This imagery is intended to be used anytime but most significantly during the first four weeks of the course. As you use "The Gift," you will become familiar with the imagery experience while learning five significant and important elements of the healing process.

As you use these imageries, your intentions will become more specific and personalized, and the outcome of the experience will be affected by your intention. So always remember to set a clear intention. Remember, your intention is what you want to achieve from this experience; it is your intended outcome. Many students have moved mountains with their session and imagery intentions.

I have used this imagery myself and have experienced great results. One Sunday morning, I woke up feeling like I had been run over by a truck. Everything in my body hurt, from the top of my head to the soles of my feet. I hurt so badly that I just wanted to cry. I sat up on the side of my bed while mustering the wherewithal to think. I was determined to make the best of it; therefore, I began to go over this imagery in my mind.

In no time at all, I was in the shower preparing for church. It was a miracle. I went to church, felt great, and had a full and complete Sunday. During the day when I felt any sensation of pain in my body I would begin to breathe out the pain and send in light and gratitude. I was amazed. I determined from that experience that I was going to participate in this imagery daily for a month. In doing so, I experienced profound results. The Spirit had promised me such results, and it was delightfully amazing to see them come to fruition.

Years ago, when I was very ill and unable to do much for myself as far as keeping up my complicated herbal, supplement, and cooking-from-scratch routine or, in my limited perception, being unable to afford going to the doctor, I prayed for help. I wanted to find something that—no matter how ill people were or how difficult their financial situations—could help them heal. This course is what the Lord gave to me in answer to that prayer, along with a very special gift titled "The Gift."

May you use this and find health, healing, wholeness, and joy as you experience the gifts of your life and the gift of unconditional love.

The intention of this imagery is to introduce the gift of breath work, the gift of focus, the gift of gratitude, the gift of light, the gift of the body, the gift of unconditional love, and most important, the gift of you.

Suggested personal intention: My intention is to receive the full benefits of this imagery experience and to become familiar with the imagery process.

Remember that these are only suggested intentions. Once you have experienced the imageries, you may want to create your own intentions and record them in your student workbook on the work sheets titled "My Imagery Sessions Intentions and Results."

A Flower Blooms

A tiny seedling, through the process of growth and time, can become a beautiful blossoming flower, fulfilling the measure of its creation and becoming all it was eternally meant to be. We are like one of these.

The intention of this imagery is to oxygenate and relax the body and to release stress, discomfort, and pain from the body while learning new and important truths. This imagery is intended to help you remember who you are.

Suggested personal intention: My intention is to be in 100 percent pure light and to relax and oxygenate my body well. I intend to release the stress and discomfort I have felt today and to receive the full benefits of this imagery session. It is my intention to remember who I am and accept my magnificence.

Birthday Present

Your birth experience is one of the most significant events of your life. Connecting to these memories and healing from your earliest misconceptions will greatly facilitate your journey to joy.

The intention of this imagery is to teach you important truths while connecting to your early birth memories. This imagery will provide an opportunity to meet some of your most significant infant needs and heal your life from those experiences.

Suggested personal intention: My intention is to be in 100 percent pure light and at a very high vibration while experiencing this imagery. I intend to participate in and receive the full benefits of this experience.

Metamorphosis

Our lives heal in the absence of fear and in the presence of unconditional love. This process begins within. It is essential to be acquainted with your inner beauty and to understand the importance and significance of self-love.

The intention of this imagery is to help you remember that life is a journey, a process of growth and change, as this title indicates.

Suggested personal intention: My intention is to be in the light and to receive the full benefits of this imagery session. I intend to accept at a deep cellular level my divine truth. I intend to accept, know, and weave into every fabric of my being that I am beautiful and that I am loved.

I Am Important

Make a difference in your life by slowing down long enough to let life flow in. Remember to take good care of yourself. You are your greatest asset.

The intention of this imagery is to help raise your vibration through breath work, meditation, and love.

Suggested personal intention: My intention is to be in the light and to receive the full benefits of this imagery. I intend to release any stress I am presently feeling with breath work and love. I intend to choose new ways of doing things that will say to myself and others that I am important and that I love to take time out for me.

Remember the Joy

The intention of this imagery is to help you remember and create the feeling of joy. We are creating a standard to return to each day, which will help you get into the feeling place of living and being in joy.

Suggested personal intention: My intention is to be in 100 percent pure light while I participate in this imagery session. I intend to receive the full benefits of this imagery experience to relax and oxygenate my body and let go of any stress I may be feeling today. I intend to connect to a wonderful joy-filled memory, one that I can remember and return to often.

Letting Go

This is a wonderful beginning imagery because of its simplicity. Learn the gift of imagery through "Letting Go."

The intention of this imagery is to experience the joy of letting go through guided imagery. Letting go of your stress and pain can be easy and joy filled.

Suggested Personal Intention: My intention is to be in 100 percent pure light while connecting to my highest truth. I intend to trust the messages and information that enter my mind. If the information is negative, I intend to let it go. If the information is positive, I intend to seal it to me as part of my divine truth.

My intention is to live, be, and experience the divine child of God that I am.

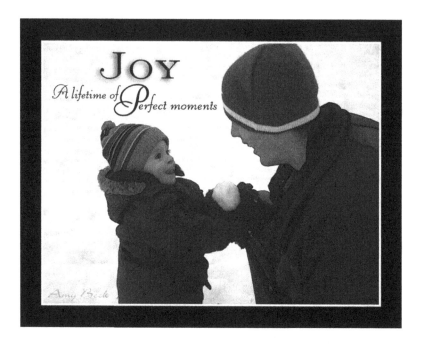

Perfect Moments I and II

The intention of these imageries is to help you capture or create a high vibration experience that will facilitate living and being in joy. These are simply moments in time. Having a repertoire of perfect moments in your mind will enable you to change your thought channel quickly, moving out of struggle and pain into joy. When you find yourself off the road, simply think of a perfect moment and move back into joy.

Begin creating your own perfect moments. When you find yourself loving what you are doing, simply frame it as a perfect moment. Focus on every element of the experience and then cement the moment in your mind. Then when you need an energy boost, think of your perfect moment long enough to shift into the feeling; soon, you will marvel at how perfectly wonderful your life is becoming.

Suggested personal intention: My intention is to be in the light and to receive the full benefits of this experience. I intend to think of my perfect moments often as I remember and acknowledge that I really have had a great and wonderful life.

Remembering Eternal Love

You may need to pause the recording at various times during this imagery to allow your memories and the experience to unfold. Use this imagery often to call forth multiple memories of love. Love is the healing power.

The intention of this imagery is to bring forth your memory of love into your present experience so that you may remember, feel, and experience love's healing energy while again remembering the love that you are.

Suggested personal intention: My intention is to return to the light from which I have come and to remember and feel the love that I am.

26

My Imagery Sessions:
Intentions and Results

Use the following worksheet found in your student workbook
for your imagery sessions. This will give you a record of your
success and help you learn the importance and significance of
the intentions you set and use.

Set and record your session intention:

Your session intention is what you want to achieve from the
experience. It is your goal, or your positive intended outcome.

_____

_____

_____

_____

_____

Things I want to remember from my session experience:

Consider recording part of your session experiences. They are
extremely significant and sometimes even sacred. I have loved

rereading the records of the sessions I have kept because they are truly some of my most joy-filled experiences.

I would encourage you to record your *positive* experiences immediately after your session because you are in a very relaxed, dream-like state and will soon forget the details of the experience.

_____
_____
_____
_____
_____
_____

Session results—Positive changes I have noticed:

Recording your session results is very beneficial. These results will be discovered *after* your imagery session, as you move through your day and throughout the course of your life. All of a sudden, you will notice that you are doing things differently or responding to a particular situation in a new way. This is what we want to look for. This is what we want to record. Look for the positive changes in your life.

When you can train your mind to focus and look for positive changes, you will indeed begin to experience a magical, joy-filled life. Furthermore, focusing on your positive results will give you the needed boost to help you stay on the road to joy, particularly if you are in a difficult or challenging life situation. If you have a record of your ability to change, you will remember, when being hit in the face with the board of life, that you have survived being hit before and that you have the skills to quickly move through it again. With each experience of moving through negative emotion, you will improve your skill level. Then the day will come when you can shift out of negative emotion in a matter of seconds or minutes, unlike your previous experiences where you stayed in them for days, months, or even years.

27
A Simple Breath-Release Clearing Process

Taking Good Care of Yourself with Breath Work

If uncomfortable emotions surface during your daily routines, acknowledge them by recording them in your emotion journal with the intention of releasing them during your next session. If you don't have the time to do a session, simply allow the emotions to surface with acceptance and love and release them with the clearing prayer or as directed below.

- Acknowledge the negative emotions you are feeling.
- Set your intention to release these negative emotions with your breath.
- Focus on the negative emotion. Take a big breath in. As you inhale, imagine the breath wrapping itself around the negative feeling. Then as you exhale, imagine the negative emotion being carried out and released with your breath.
- Continue this process until you feel relief. As you are working this process, new negative feelings

will often enter your mind as the original ones are released. Continue releasing until you are in a balanced state.

28

Journey to Joy Toolbox

The Journey to Joy Toolbox is a quick-reference review of some of the tools covered in the course. These tools are to be used when you want to raise your vibration, shift out of negative energy, or stay focused on the positive aspects of your life. Using these tools and becoming adept with them will help you enjoy your journey through life.

1. **Prayer.** Prayer is a great vehicle to help you glide through life. Are you using it to its fullest capacity, or are you just honking your horn to announce to God that you're checking in? Remember, God will answer any question you ask. Your part is to let go of your fears and trust and believe the thoughts that come into your mind. Set your intention that you will see and know the ways God is answering your prayers. Prayer is your number one tool.

2. **Journey to Joy Course Imageries**. This is one of your greatest clearing and creating tools. Imageries give your life the message on every level that this is what is wanted. Imagery is the doorway to help you

connect to the greatest part of you, and it is a process that will help develop your spiritual sight. Use the imageries in this course often, and with each use they will move you one step closer to experiencing a joy-filled, happy life.

3. **Vibration Sensor.** Everyone has a vibration sensor. Attune yourself to this marvelous tool and use it moment by moment to live by. When you think positive thoughts, you will feel up and happy. When you think negative thoughts, you will feel down. This is an indication of the vibration of your thoughts. You feel what you feel because you think what you think. If you don't like how you are feeling, change your thoughts. Negative feelings are a message of love. They will remind you to change your direction.

4. **Breath Work.** If you want to experience a joy–filled, happy life, begin by adding life to your joy—*breathe*. Breath work is a great clearing and releasing tool. Remember, you can't be in negative emotion while breathing properly. Breath work is the key that unlocks the door to the subconscious realm, where your negative patterns and beliefs are stored. Breath marks the beginning of life. It can also mark the beginning of your new life.

5. **The Eight-Step Process.** The eight-step process is a tool to help you discover your patterns and beliefs, learn from the opposition your beliefs created, and then eliminate and reframe the core beliefs you just discovered. The eight-step process is a simple formula that will help bring about great change in your life. This process is taught and practiced in

the live Journey to Joy workshops, seminars, and courses.

6. **Imagery, Meditation, and Visualization.** This is the creation process. Create daily with the powerful tool of visualization. Remember that when using imagery to create, you are creating your blueprint on every level of your being. Every part of your life is getting a picture of what you want.

7. **Daily Intentions.** Setting daily intentions is like laying out a smooth road for your day to run on. It is the equivalent of your journey's map. When you begin setting intentions, you begin to become the director of your life.

8. **Affirmations.** Raise your vibration by stating positive affirmations. Go on an affirmation drive or walk, and listen to the recorded affirmations. Do an affirmation dance, thinking, "I am in joy." Spend your thought time wisely.

9. **Because Tracks.** This is a digging tool used to help you discover your hidden roadblocks. Pay attention to resistance. Remember, a roadblock is merely information surfacing, or an indication of your resistance. The Because Tracks will help you identify what you are feeling at deeper levels.

10. **Focus.** Focus your thoughts on what you want, not on what you don't want. Focus is your directional system bringing into your life what you are thinking about. Focus coupled with emotion increases the power of the magnetic pull. Think of how we get a child to change focus. We help him put his attention

on something else. When we are triggered, we are often experiencing the misconceptions of childhood again. Change your focus to get out of the energy of the moment until you have the time to clear the patterns and bring them to resolution. When you refocus, put your attention on what you want instead.

11. **Gratitude.** Opposition is our greatest teacher. When we get the lesson, the teacher will disappear. Gratitude for your growth is a great indication that you are there, that you got what the teacher was trying to teach you. Gratitude is a very high vibration and is the predecessor to joy. Step into it, and you will feel the power of it. This is when you bring your masterpiece into view. Stand back and look in gratitude at the wonder of what you have learned and the miracle of your life's creations.

12. **Love.** Love is the power that heals lives. Loving yourself is your greatest mission. Focus on memories of love, laughter, and joy. Bring these memories to the surface with the intention of experiencing them again and again. Love *every* aspect of your journey through life, even "your enemy" or the negative experiences you have gone through. When you bring in love, you bring in healing energy. Do a little something every day that says to your body and your life, "I love you."

13. **Emotion Journal.** An emotion journal can be for writing both positive and negative emotions. Recording your positive emotions will help you stay on the road to joy. You will want to review these writings often. Recording your negative emotions

is a way to help you prepare for your next clearing session, or you may simply intend to let them go as you write them down. This is a great way to release.

14. **Presleep Count-Off with Imagery.** Every night before you go off to sleep, say a positive statement of your choice while imagining the end results. In order to stay awake and not lose count before you do drop off to sleep, press down a finger with each repetition of the targeted phrase until you have completed at least ten repetitions. Presleep is a powerful time for positive self-programming. You will feel the results the next day.

15. **Perfect Questions.** Start your day off by asking a few simple questions, such as, "What would I be better with today?" Listen for the response and then act upon the information. Another perfect question that will absolutely transform your life is to ask God, "What would you like me to do today?" This question is evidence of your desire to surrender your heart to Him. When someone gives something away, they no longer possess it, but when you give your life to God, you get it back with so much more, and oh, the joy this brings.

16. **Daily D.** Sit in the sunshine every day for at least fifteen minutes, barefoot if possible. Nature is very cleansing and healing. The best times are in the early morning hours or late evening, around sunset. Sit in the sun that warms you, not heats you. The first and last hours of sunlight have no UV rays. You may use this time to multitask, perhaps listening to the imageries, saying your affirmations, or writing

in your journal while soaking up the healing rays of the sun.

17. **Take Time Out for You.** If you want to have a joy-filled life, you will realize that you are the only one who can make that happen. Establishing happiness and joy is an inside job, not an outside one. If you keep looking to others to make you happy, you will never find happiness because it is found in the heart. You are the one behind that powerful mind. You are the one who makes all the "thought choices." Choose to be happy on a daily basis; choose to do something every day that will bring you joy and peace. Begin today by taking care of your greatest tool, *yourself.*

18. **A Power Shower.** This utilizes visualization, affirmations, and body movement to create a powerful, high-energy experience. Turn something you do every day into a powerful tool that will help you keep your focus and get into the feeling place of what you want.

19. **Framing a Perfect Moment.** Frame moments in your life when you are feeling positive and happy as "perfect moments." Pay attention to every detail of the experience. Ask yourself, "What makes this moment wonderful?" When you frame it as a perfect moment, you will have a strong memory to return to when you are in need of a positive lift.

20. **Smile Breath.** This is a great tool to lift your vibration. Take a big breath in and then smile the biggest, cheesiest grin you can muster. When you are at the top of the breath and the top of the

smile, hold it for a few seconds while noticing your feelings, and then relax your smile and release the breath at the same time. Repeat this at least ten times. Visualize when you do this little exercise that every cell in your body is smiling with you.

21. **One Thought Higher.** When you find yourself in a challenging life situation and your thoughts are growling at you, think, *Can I think one thought higher than this one?* Then ponder your situation for a moment, trying to pull up a thought that will make you feel a little better than the last one did. When you raise your vibration a little with that thought, then do it again and again and continue to raise your thoughts one step at a time until you are out of the grumbles and into gratitude and joy.

These techniques and tools are also taught in the live Journey to Joy workshops, courses, and seminars.

Journey to Joy: A Course about Living and Being in Joy
Written and Produced by:
Tannie Bennett
Master Rapid-Eye Practitioner, Certified Clinical Hypnosis,
Spiritual Teacher & Coach, Joy Master

29
Rapid-Eye Technology

An Introduction to the Possibilities

Rapid-eye is an effective release process that helps you to let go of your recorded misconceptions, negative beliefs, and stress. Rapid-eye technology, or RET, is a gift to our world. Its founder, Dr. Ranae Johnson, was inspired in the creation of this work. Rapid-eye technology is a divine process that is solidly based in science and backed by years of research and experience. The intention of this amazing process is to relieve stress and to help change your core programming.

I discovered rapid eye as an answer to my own personal prayers for help. I had spent many years struggling with life. When I had had enough, I opened myself to be led, and this is where life took me.

My initial interest in rapid eye was to help myself and my family, but it quickly extended to others as I became acquainted with the power and magnitude of this incredible process. Each and every session brought joy. In my early beginning, I was surprised at the potential that was before me. The possibilities were far-reaching, but it took some time and experience with it to fully comprehend its magnitude.

Allow me to share one of my earliest experiences as a rapid-eye practitioner. A sweet lady came to my office for a session. She was totally stressed and overwhelmed with life. I was personally acquainted with this woman, and I looked at her and thought, *Wow, this is definitely not one of your best days.* In fact, she looked totally beat up by life. Her energy was scattered, her complexion was splotchy and red, and her face and jaw appeared out of alignment.

As I worked on her, I started to blink. In rapid eye, that is one of the client's jobs, but I was blinking because I could hardly believe what I was witnessing. Her face and skin began to change; her complexion turned a beautiful pink. Then as I turned her focus to her beauty, talents, and gifts, her true self began to emerge. The change after one session was incredible. I thought, *Wow, this is amazing.*

A few short minutes after this client arrived home, I received a call from her sister, who said, "Tannie, what did you do to Sarah? She looks fantastic!" The change was noticed by her entire family, and needless to say I have had many opportunities to serve that family because of the results they saw in Sarah.

I have loved seeing the results this process has brought into people's lives, but most significantly I have loved the changes it has brought into my own. I have been very dedicated to my own clearing. Not a day has passed since I began my healing journey that I have not felt the effects of this incredible process in some form or another in my life. I have learned that I no longer have to feel bad, mad, sad, depressed, angry, frustrated, crazy, lonely, scared, worried, anxious, or any other negative emotion. I now have a tool to help me through these experiences and feel joy. The minute I feel something come up, I have a tool to assist me. I can now move in and out of these experiences quickly and enjoy lasting change as a result. I love what I teach and practice.

The most significant thing to remember is that change, lasting change, takes time. Remember that and be kind to yourself as you begin the process of change. You won't have to look any further because this process works; it really works.

In my early beginnings, I realized that I could not even practice this process on another without releasing energy. When you begin the rapid-eye process, you begin to release. It works that well.

RET's founder, Dr. Ranae Johnson, has an incredible personal story, which is eloquently told in part in her book *Winter's Flower.* Ranae had an autistic child during a time when little was known about autism. While searching for something to help her child, she learned a great deal about the brain—what worked and what didn't. This became the foundation of her work. At one point Ranae took time out for a personal spiritual retreat, and it was during this time that she received as a gift from the Spirit the rapid-eye model. Ranae has spent years developing the process into the incredible tool we have today. Each year, the model is expanded because of the research and experiences of her students and research teams. Now as never before, science and society are catching up to the vision she has had for more than three decades.

Within the rapid-eye model are many tools to effectively assist in the release process. These tools consist of the basic rapid-eye process, along with imagery, energy work, breath work, and more.

For the practitioner, the process begins by creating a rapport with clients, helping them to feel comfortable and informing them of what they can expect. We discuss why you are here and what you hope to achieve from your sessions. From this information, we set a basic intention. This is a very important part of the process because an intention is the track your session will run on. It is all about what you want, including what you want to achieve from your sessions. It can even include how fast you want to go. For example, an intention might look something like this: "My intention is to clear in divine order the most significant core patterns that are affecting my life in a negative way—to clear all attachments, all parts, and all altered phrases of these patterns. It is my intention to clear with grace and ease in the time we have allotted and to leave feeling light and joy filled."

Or, if you have in mind a particular pattern or issue you want to clear, you may say, "My intention is to clear, from a 100 percent pure light level, (state the pattern or issue) with grace and ease, clearing all attachments and parts, to gain understanding of this experience in my life and to quickly notice the results of this session in my life."

An intention can be whatever you want to achieve from your session. As you become familiar with this experience, you will then be able to formulate your own intentions and become very specific in them. I have heard some very interesting intentions and as a result have had some very interesting and wonderful sessions. Let your inner light guide you in this. Ponder before your session what your intention will be. Please keep in mind the time element.

After your intention is set, we then begin the release work process. In the rapid-eye model, it is not necessary to give detailed stories about your personal life. All we need is basic information and basic emotion. From this, we are able to complete the process of releasing negative emotions and core beliefs. In fact, we are able to release more patterns with fewer stories because we have more time available for the release work process. Some basic information is required, and if the practitioner needs more information, he or she will ask. It is quite surprising how little you need to divulge to have this process work effectively. It could work even if nothing was said and only a basic intention was set, although I would not encourage that.

Many clients are fearful about what they are going to find when they begin. There is no need to worry: the client sets the pace. It is up to you how fast and how far you go, and you will never release anything you are not ready for. After you have a few successful release sessions, you become very eager to get everything out because it feels so good.

The RET model has many safeguards built into it so that the release work is never more than you can handle. We can slow it down or speed it up—whatever suits the intention or comfort of the client. This work is very client friendly. You are in the driver's seat, and we as practitioners are mere tour guides who assist by knowing where to go, how to get there, and what to do when we arrive. The client always chooses the intention and the speed. The rapid-eye practitioner may assist and recommend, if help is needed.

The rapid-eye model simulates REM sleep. Sleep is your body's natural healing time, and it is during this period that the body sorts and stores the information it has been given in a single day. If during the course of the day an individual experienced trauma, the brain has a message to protect and store this information, and this experience is then locked in cellular memory as a stored trauma. It is during your REM sleep, when the brain is pulsating in the alpha, theta, or delta modes, that these files, this information, can be opened and released. Through verbal cues, the trauma, memories, and emotions are able to surface and be released while the client is fully conscious and awake. There is resolution in nearly every session.

The rapid-eye model goes first to the core of the problem. When the core is reached, all forming attachments to this problem are subsequently released as well. The proof is then found in the life changes the client experiences. You will feel these changes in your life.

The changes are often subtle because our established patterns are to pay more attention to what feels bad than to what feels good. When we feel good, our mind quickly heads in the direction of the next problem, but you will feel change. Clients who are extremely motivated and focused seem to experience the most profound results. Remember, as I mentioned before, you are in the driver's seat. Your focused, powerful intention will determine whether you receive focused, powerful results.

Throughout the process, you will be taught techniques to assist in self-care. The only time these techniques do not work is when the client forgets to use them. There are many tools to assist you. Once these tools are mastered, you will be in a position to assist those around you, improving our world one life at a time.

We are not taught, as we go through life, how to handle stress. We are taught to buck up, be tough, and be a man. I remember years ago even hearing my husband, mostly in jest, tell our young daughters, "Be a man."

Think about your life. What techniques were you taught to handle your stress? What techniques do you know now to help you handle stress? Can they shift you from panic, fear, and distress in a matter of seconds or minutes? This is what you will learn as you go through this course.

I will not be teaching the rapid-eye process in the Journey to Joy course, but I will teach you techniques that you can use at home to receive amazing results.

One particular experience I had with using these tools was quite remarkable. I was visiting my daughter, who was living away from home at the time. That evening, her phone rang. Being quite late at night, I thought it was my husband calling to say good night. I went into her bedroom to check to see who was on the phone, and I sat down on her bed to listen. I quickly surmised that it wasn't her dad. I listened as she began consoling someone on the other end of the line. She kept repeating herself, evidence that she was having a bit of a struggle. I asked her if I could listen and perhaps help out. She agreed, so I picked up the other line. I then became very aware of why she was repeating herself. On the other end of the line was a young man who had lost his prestigious job and his girlfriend all in the same day. It was more than he could handle. All we heard was uncontrollable sobbing.

I signaled to Christie to use one of our stress-release techniques that she knew. She asked this young man if he would try something for her, and he agreed. She then coached him in the process, and as soon as he applied the technique, his sobbing sputtered to a halt. It was amazing, and Christie was much relieved, not to mention how much better the young man felt. I personally have used rapid eye or the techniques taught in the course nearly every day to move out of stress or assist someone else out of stress.

One afternoon as I was flying home from Texas, I was seated by a beautiful young woman who was on her way to visit her college roommate of years past. The plane took off in somewhat dismal weather. As we ascended, the plane began to jerk and move with the air turbulence we were flying into. This was very unnerving to this young woman. She grabbed my arm and began to squeeze. So I whipped out my toolbox, figuratively speaking, and shared with her one of the techniques. Within seconds, she released her grip and relaxed. The woman on the other side of her looked at me in awe and asked, "Now what did you just do?"

I love having these tools to assist my family and those around me. I have many stories I could share as a result of this fantastic program. This process is definitely something everyone could benefit from. The techniques are easy. They only require confidence, training, and experience in using them.

This is only a beginning. The best is yet to come as you embark on this wonderful journey of improving your life and releasing your stress one day at a time.

*For more information about Rapid-Eye Technology, visit the Rapid Eye Institute website at http://rapideyetechnology.com.

Part **IV**

Journey to Joy Stories

30
Annabelle's Trial

The intentions of the Journey to Joy stories are to captivate and bring joy while supporting the principles found within the course material.

The objective of this story is to illustrate that going through the school of opposition and choice is the path we chose to help us to become all we were meant to be.

Once there lived a beautiful fairy princess who delighted in all the creations of God. Her responsibility was to scan the forest kingdom in search of anything that was out of order with God's natural laws. When she happened upon a situation in question, she would report her findings to her father, the king. He would in turn bring it to the attention of the elders. Then it was their decision whether to change the misdeed or leave it for natural consequences.

While flying through the forest one day, the fairy princess observed something very interesting. It appeared to be a lost child. The child was not a fairy child, for fairy children never lose their way. Their kingdom was the forest, and their instincts were so well developed that they always knew exactly where they were. This was a human child. The fairy princess did not know the age of the child, for she knew not the time of man. The time of fairies and the time of man differed greatly. The child seemed very small in comparison to the humans the princess had seen in times past.

The child was leaning heavily on a tree, weeping bitterly, and was in quite a state of anxiety. The surrounding plants had called for the princess to come and help. When the princess arrived, she circled the child, looking for the reason of her distress. The plants had told her that she appeared lost, but the princess knew that other things could have caused the child's distress, perhaps an injury or something else. As she circled, she found nothing to indicate the cause of the child's sorrow.

Hmmm, she pondered. *What shall I do? We don't often reveal ourselves to humans, but for the sake of this poor child I feel I must.*

The fairy princess flew toward the child's face, staying back a bit so as not to totally frighten her. She called to the child, "Hello, my young friend." The child heard the voice and stopped to look, looking right past the fairy princess. She was looking for a human. She looked all around the forest and, not seeing anything, again began to weep.

"Hello, my young friend," the fairy princess repeated. "It is I, the fairy princess Adorahlee."

Adorahlee flew around so the young child could see her. The child caught sight of her and was pleased with what she saw. She put out her hand in a gesture for the princess to land. Of course, Adorahlee obliged.

"What is the problem, my young friend? Can I help you find your way home?"

"No, I am not lost. I ran away from my home, and I am not going back! I hate my home. All my parents do is fight with each other, and I don't want to be a part of it. I will live in the forest with you and all the animals. I will be fine. I'm not sure how, but I will make it. All I know is that I am not going back!"

"Child, you are very young to live alone in the forest," Adorahlee replied. "There are dangers here of which you are unaware. Could you possibly reconsider your decision? I am sure there are other alternatives."

"If there are, I don't know them," the child said. "I have asked my parents many times to stop fighting. I have prayed that they would stop, yet they do not hear my words. They don't know what this is doing to my heart. It is breaking my heart! I love them so. I don't like this at all. I figure if they don't hear me, I might as well not be there. So I decided to run away. I have packed a few things I thought I would need."

"Well, if this is what you want, why do you sorrow so?"

"I sorrow for my little brother. I left him with them. I knew I could take care of myself. I also knew I could not take care of him. So I left him, and I hear his cries. He is crying for me to come home. I don't know what to do. I don't want to leave him there with all that fighting; I know that it is breaking his heart too."

"My parents feel we are too little to know what is going on, yet they don't know that we feel all they feel. My brother, though he is only a baby, knows exactly what is going on. He sorrows as I do. He cries every night till he falls asleep exhausted. I am at a loss for what to do. I don't want to go back, yet I don't want to go forward without Adam. Adam is a baby. I must go back to get him. Fairy princess, will you help me take care of my little baby brother? I know I could do it with your help."

"Oh, my, that is quite a request," Adorahlee said. "I will have to bring the matter before the king and the elders. I cannot make such a decision on my own, for it is law that we do not interfere with the lives of men. We are the keepers of the forest. That's our stewardship."

"Can we ... go now to ask them?" the young child asked slowly.

"Well, I suppose. That is probably the best thing to do, for I have never had such a situation as this. Please follow me the best you can. I will go slowly for your sake."

The princess Adorahlee and the young child headed off through the woods.

"By the way, child, what is your title? What do they call you?"

"My name is Annabelle. That is my birth name, yet my family calls me Anna."

"What name would you like me to use to introduce you to the king?"

"Please call me Annabelle. That was the name of my beloved grandmother who is now in heaven. I do miss her so. If she were still here, I would be with her right now, and Adam too."

"Okay, Annabelle, we are almost there. Please do not say anything to the king unless the king speaks directly to you. I will be your mediator for the king. You will be speaking to me. Is that understood?"

"Yes, I understand."

Annabelle found the thought of going before the fairy king and the council of elders quite exciting. She knew none of her friends would have had such an adventure. She was also excited to think of the possibility of getting help for Adam.

Adorahlee approached the king and bowed before him.

"Father, I have found a matter in the forest of great concern to me, and I need your wisdom and advice."

"Go ahead, child."

"Father, I know it is not our custom to interfere with the matters of men, but I have found a small child in great distress and she needs our help. She ran away from her home because of the great contention there, and she refuses to return. Her sorrow comes from the fact that her baby brother is left behind; she hears his call and doesn't know what to do. The baby is crying for her to return. She wants to get him, but she fears she cannot take care of him by herself and needs our help. Can we help her, Father?"

"Adorahlee! This is a matter of great concern! You have interfered with man already. I know your heart sorrows for the distressed child, but mankind is not our stewardship; the forest is. What would you have me do, child?"

"Oh, Father, I don't know. It saddened me so to hear her weeping. It was the forest trees and animals that called me to help her. All I knew to do was to bring her here for your wisdom and advice."

"Hmmm," the king said. "I will call a counsel, and then I will report to you our decision. Take the child back to where you found her and tell her she will hear from you soon."

Adorahlee took Annabelle back to her tree and instructed the nearby animals to watch over her and keep her safe. She was to stay there until Adorahlee returned.

Annabelle sorrowed at this. She had heard of fairies and their magic and knew she could get the help she needed, or at least she was hopeful.

Annabelle settled down in the soft grass to sleep for the night. She wrapped the blanket she had brought around her, yet she couldn't sleep. She could hear Adam crying.

"Oh, what shall I do? What shall I do? If I return to get him, I could get caught and boy the trouble I would be in then. I don't want to face that, yet I can't stand to hear him cry any longer."

She told the trees her plan and asked them to please tell Adorahlee. She said, "I will be back with Adam tomorrow if all goes well. I will leave all my wares here so I can bring Adam's things." She then took off through the woods and headed for home.

When she arrived home, it was quiet. "Wow! I haven't heard that in a while. I guess Dad is not home yet or Mother is not." She crept up to the window to look in. Everything was still. She went around to the back of the house to look in the windows there. The lights were on, yet still she saw no one. "I guess they all must be upstairs," she said. She listened for the baby to cry, but she heard nothing. "Oh, man, I guess I am going to have to go inside." She took a big breath in and headed for the front door, but it was locked. "Mom and Dad never lock the door," she said. "This is strange. I'll get the key." She knew where it was hidden, but to her surprise it wasn't there.

"Well, great. Now what am I to do? I know—a window. I'll go through the upstairs window. Surely they would not lock the windows."

She climbed up the tree by her bedroom window and jumped to the roof. She scampered down the trellis to her window and tried to open it. It was locked too; her bedroom light was off, and so was Adam's. She couldn't see anything at all, and she saw no sign of anybody being home.

Well, now I am in a pickle, she thought. *What should I do?* She tried to tune in to Adam, but she couldn't connect with him. She jumped back to the tree and sat perched there, pondering her next action. *I don't know where they are. I wonder if they have gone to look for me. I wonder if they know I'm gone.*

This surprised her; she felt she was invisible to her parents. *Do they know I am gone?* She enjoyed the thought of her parents looking for her. It caused her to feel that maybe they loved her after all. She decided to crawl down out of the tree to check the garage and see if the car was missing. It was. "That's it. That's where they have gone. They have gone to look for me." She was hopeful. The thought that she was missed brought her joy. She knew Adam missed her, but she didn't think her parents cared for anything but fighting because that's all they did.

Dad would come home, and the fighting would begin. She would see her mother crying on the bed, day after day. She would try to help, yet she was small and did not know what to do other than pray that her mom and dad would stop. But they never did.

Annabelle then saw lights coming up the drive. She ran to hide in the forest. She planned to listen to see if she could learn anything as they got out of the car.

When the car pulled up and the passengers got out, to her surprise, it was not her parents at all. It was not even her family.

"What are they doing at my house?" She watched as the family hurried into the house. They unlocked the door and went in.

"They have a key to my house! Why would they have a key to my house? I am going to get to the bottom of this." She ran to the front door and rang the bell.

"I'll get it, honey," she heard a soft, kind voice remark. The door opened, and there in her house stood a kind and gentle man who said, "Well hello, Annabelle. We have been waiting for you. Do come in."

Annabelle walked in and demanded to know where her family was.

"We are your new family. We are here to replace your old, fighting one. You prayed for a change, and we are it. Your bedroom is upstairs. It's just like you left it, and—oh, Adam is in his room. We knew you would want to keep him too, so we did. But we got rid of your mom and dad. We knew you were sick and tired of them, so they are gone and now you don't ever have to worry about them again. We are your new family. You still have your bed, all your things, Adam, and now a new set of parents who will love and adore you. Shall I begin to love and adore you now, or would you like to get a good night's rest tonight and start tomorrow? I know you have had quite the day in the forest. What shall it be?"

Annabelle was stunned. New parents? What a concept! Maybe she did not need the fairies' help after all. She decided to go to bed and start afresh the next day.

"That would be fine," her new dad said. "Good night, honey. Let me at least go and tuck you in bed and tell you a bedtime story. How does that sound?"

"Um, fine, I guess," Annabelle answered.

The new dad followed her into her room, tucked her into bed, and told her a wonderful bedtime story. Then she saw her new mother standing in the doorway with Adam in her arms.

"Annabelle, someone wants to tell you good night."

There in her arms was baby Adam, smiling sweetly. Mom walked over to Annabelle and bent down so she could give Adam a kiss good night. Annabelle was amazed. Adam seemed so calm and happy.

The new mom left and said, "Good night, honey. I love you so much. Have a good night's sleep. Tomorrow I am fixing your favorite for breakfast—blueberry waffles."

Annabelle didn't remember that as her favorite, yet it sounded great. She sure would give it a try. She then snuggled in for a good night's sleep.

The next morning she awoke to the sounds of the baby giggling and the smell of something wonderful cooking in the kitchen. She jumped out of bed, got dressed, and ran down the stairs to the kitchen. Sure enough, there was Adam sitting in his high chair and the table all set with the most glorious breakfast one could imagine—beautiful, fat blueberry waffles with whipped cream and a huge plate of crispy bacon.

Oh, man, this must be a dream, Annabelle thought as she sat down to eat.

"Wait just a moment, dear," her mom said. "Dad is not here, and we always eat together. Father, breakfast is ready now. Do come down."

Annabelle smiled at baby Adam and thought, *Adam, this is great! I don't know how we did it, but look, no more fighting parents.* Adam smiled at Annabelle, knowing just what she was thinking.

Father entered the room.

"Mother, you have done it again. Kids, look at this great breakfast. Isn't Mom the best?"

He then went over to give her a big kiss and a huge good morning hug. Annabelle smiled inside herself. Now this is the way every family should be. They should always be kind and love each other and appreciate all the good things they do. Annabelle ate, thanked her mom for the delicious breakfast, and got up to help her with the dishes.

"No, no, honey. I'll take care of these. You just go pick up your room and then go off to play. I know Chelsea would love to play with you today."

Annabelle was baffled. Before, she always had to fight to be able to go anywhere. She really loved this new situation. *I don't even miss my old mom and dad,* she thought. She hurried upstairs to pick up her room. She quickly put all her toys away and then ran out to play.

Time passed. Annabelle's life was wonderful. She never missed the fighting, and she rarely thought of her old mom and dad. Adam seemed happy too.

"This is the life," Annabelle sighed.

One day, as Annabelle was off playing in the woods, she happened upon the old tree where she had first met the fairy princess. There, in the same place, was all the stuff she left the day she ran away.

"Oh, my, I forgot all about my things. I guess I don't have to worry about that now. I am happy, and so is Adam. I would like to at least tell the fairy princess of my good fortune."

She remembered that the tree had called to Adorahlee before, so she put her hand on the tree and asked, "Please, tree, could you call the fairy princess to me? I would like to tell her of my good fortune."

Soon, there before her was the fairy princess.

"Well, hello, Annabelle. How do you like your new family?" the fairy princess asked.

"My new family—how did you know about my new family?" Annabelle asked. "Ahhh … it was you! You were the ones who gave me my new family, weren't you?"

"It was not I; it was the king and the council who granted you this fine new family. How's it going?"

"I love them. It is so nice to have peace and to have a home filled with love. My new mom is great. She is a fabulous cook, and she reads me stories! She even sits down on the floor and plays with baby Adam. He is quite happy too. But I would like to know where my old parents are. Are they still fighting, or are they divorced by now? I was so sick of hearing the threat of divorce. Dad was always asking me who I would like to go with if they got divorced—him or Mom. I did not want to go with either of them. That is why I ran away. And now I still do not have to go with either of them. Adam and I are both really happy. What a wonderful gift you gave me. Thank you so much. Can I go thank the king and the council myself, or would it be best if you just gave them the message?"

"No," Adorahlee replied. "This time I think it would be best if you spoke to the king yourself. He can answer all your questions. Follow me."

Annabelle followed the fairy princess through the woods, and Adorahlee presented her to the king. Upon entering the presence of the king, Annabelle bowed in respect to him. The king invited her to be seated.

"Well, Annabelle, how is the new family?"

"Oh, good king, I want to thank you so much for this kind deed. It is so wonderful to live with a loving family and not one that's always fighting. My sweet baby Adam seems so happy too. He hardly ever cries anymore. Our new mother is so good to him. And well, we both are just as happy as we can be. Thank you so much. This is more than I could ever ask for. Please forgive me for taking so long to thank you. I didn't know it was you who arranged this for me. Thank you!"

Annabelle again bowed before the king to thank him.

The good king smiled.

"That is good, but do you know the cost of this gift you received?"

"Cost? No one mentioned cost to me. What do you mean by cost?"

"Annabelle, this gift was given with a great cost to you and your little brother."

"Cost, what cost? What must I pay? I have no money, good King. Don't you think you should have told me of this before now so that I might have bargained with you, or at least known about it so I could have chosen?"

"Annabelle, you did choose. You have been praying for a different family for a long time, and you have been praying for a happy home."

"Yes, I wanted that, but at what expense did I get these things?" Annabelle began to fear the consequences of her actions.

"Oh, my, what did I do? What did I do? All I wanted was to be happy and to have a happy home. Is that too much to ask?"

"No, that's not too much to ask," the king answered. "But for every action there is a consequence."

"What is the consequence? Can I go back if I do not like the consequence of my actions?"

"Well, now, we will have to see. First, let me spell out the consequence of the choice you have made. Adorahlee, please bring me the magic looking glass."

Adorahlee brought her father a beautiful handheld mirror set in gold, with beautiful flowers and vines etched into it. Annabelle had never seen anything of such great beauty and value. The mirror was very large; it appeared to be made for man, not for fairies. Annabelle waited to see what was to happen next.

Adorahlee placed the mirror in front of Annabelle. She took hold of the handle and saw her reflection in the glass.

"Annabelle, the mirror is magic and will tell you of your future. What would you like to see—the future with your old family or the future with your new?"

"I would like to see the future with my new family," she answered. "I do love them so."

Annabelle was excited to see her future with her new family for she knew it was going to be great. She knew she was going to have a very happy life. Her future flew before her with great speed. She saw her whole life in what appeared to be moments. She saw herself up until the time of her death.

"Wow. That was a surprise," she said when it was finished.

"What was a surprise?" the king asked.

"My life. I felt I would have had such a fantastic life with this wonderful family, but in my later years, I didn't really amount to much. My life seemed pretty boring and uneventful. Hmm, may I see my life with my old family?"

"Why, certainly, Annabelle. That is why you are here."

Annabelle watched her life of trial in amazement. "Wow, that's a surprise," she said as she watched. "Hmm … wow … cool … that's neat!" When it was finished, she looked at the king and said, "I don't understand. Why is my difficult life so much better at the end than my easy life? My whole family is so strong, and look at the wonderful things that we were all able to accomplish! I grew up in a horrible situation, and yet look at how wonderful things turned out. I don't get it. Why is this one so great and the one that I thought was so great actually so boring and unsuccessful?"

"Well," the king began, "the opposition you faced when you were small caused great growth in you. You became convinced that you were not going to repeat the mistakes your parents made. This trial made you determined to change things for your family and your children. You grew because of the opposition you had to face. You became great because of the choices you made in the face of the very opposition you wanted out of so badly as a child. It caused a burning within your soul to rise above all of your trials. You knew you had it in you to change things, and you indeed did.

"In your new family, you grew up in ease and comfort. This caused you to become lazy and never try for anything. For your entire life, you had all the comforts you could have ever wished for. You never had to struggle. Life was easy. You did not become what you had the potential to become because you never had to struggle and try. So you dwindled to the state you saw in your first future. That is the cost I was talking about. Ease caused you to be less than you could have been, while opposition helped you to grow and become strong and mighty. You became a great influence for good because of the trials you went through as a child."

"Oh," she sighed. "I do not want to go back. It was too hard. Can I just try really hard to make more of myself?"

"No, my sweet Annabelle. That is not how it works. Opposition is the force that makes one strong. When the opposition is removed, so is the strength. Many have desired to grow without opposition. They do a little, and then the growing stops. It is quite like physical exercise—the muscles must have resistance to grow strong."

"Oh, man, I had no idea I was giving up so much," Annabelle said. "I had a wonderful future with my old family, yet for me as a child, the pain seemed to last forever."

"But it did not last forever, did it?" the king asked. "Growth and strength are elements that take time. All life desires ease and joy, yet it is the opposition that causes the constant upward movement."

"Many have learned the gift of opposition," he continued. "They no longer look at it as the enemy. They, while in the midst of opposition, are able to look for the good. This quality, too, takes time to develop. Yet if you had this knowledge in your first childhood, you might have been able to endure it longer."

"Oh, what am I to do?" Annabelle asked. "I do not want to give up so much of my future for a soft and easy childhood. Yet I am still young, and I fear going back. I don't think I have the strength to endure it all."

"You have the strength, for you have seen yourself in the future. You made it very nicely."

"Oh, right. I guess I did, didn't I?"

Annabelle took in a big deep breath. *Well, if I did it once, I can do it again*, she thought. "Good King, may I still make a choice of the future and life I desire?"

"Why, certainly child, that is why you are here, to decide the path you want to take. You still have the choice. You are young; you may make a new choice anytime."

"Well," she said, "I think I want to go back to my old life. I know it will be hard, yet I know Adam and I are going to make it. I have seen us both. I want the future of my old life. I do not want to live a life of little growth, for I feel unsatisfied with that path. I know I have great potential, and I desire to become all that I can be."

"That is good, my sweet Annabelle," the king said, "for that is the path that you decided upon long before your birth. It is good that again you are choosing to receive great growth.

"You are an amazing young lady. You have a great and glorious future. You will live a wonderful life of service, and your life will affect the lives of millions. Go now; return to your home and remember that you have within you all you need to make it through your trials. You too are a princess. Do not forget that."

Annabelle left the fairy king to return to her home. She became determined to make it. She was determined to be there for Adam, to love him, and to take care of him the best she could.

On her way home, Annabelle thought, *We are going to be great someday, Adam, and this is how we are going to do it. We are going to go through the school of opposition and choice, and we will make it!*

She pondered as she walked home through the woods. "I will focus on my greatness, not my pain."

Instantly her burden lightened.

31
Mirror, Mirror

The objective of this story is to help you see within yourself what is so easily seen in others.

Once upon a time, not long ago, a beautiful princess lived with her handsome prince. They lived in a small palace not far from the king. They were very happy in their little palace. They worked and played together each and every day.

As time passed, they started a family of their own. Their family meant the world to them. They loved their children deeply. They played and worked together, teaching them all about life.

Then one day, a change began to take place in the little palace. The prince seemed to grow weary of his position as prince. The princess noticed these subtle changes in him, and she began to worry a bit—not too much at first. She thought he might just be going through something typical for his age.

The phase lasted much longer than was comfortable for the princess. The prince began to show anger and started to act unkindly toward the children. He was often away from home for long periods of time without telling the princess where he was going or when to expect his return. This change became quite disturbing to the princess.

Needing advice, the princess decided to go visit her father, the king. He was pleased to see the princess and the children, as he was each time they came to visit. But this time he became concerned when he realized that the prince was not journeying with them.

"Father, may I have a word with you in private?" the princess asked.

"Why, certainly, my dear. Let's retire to the study. I have been quite eager to show you the most recent addition to my collection."

They left for the study, and the children ran out to play. Upon reaching the study, the king asked, "Sweetheart, where is the prince?"

"That is the reason I have come, Father," she answered. "I don't know what to do. There have been changes taking place in him, and I am quite puzzled by his behavior." She then proceeded to expound on the prince's behavior.

"Hmm ... how very interesting," the king replied. "And just how long has this been going on?" he asked.

"Well, to be honest, I'm not quite sure," the princess answered. "I noticed it quite a while ago but felt it was probably just me, so I ignored it and kept doing my daily activities. Then he began to have anger problems, and they grew. I don't even know the cause of his anger. He never talks to me anymore, and he is often gone for very long periods of times. Oh, Father, what am I to do? My beautiful dream family is disappearing right before my eyes."

"Now, dear, don't be dismayed. All is well."

"Well, it certainly doesn't look or feel well," the princess remarked. "Father, I'm worried about him. I'm worried about the children and me. I don't want to live the rest of my life alone."

"And what gave you the idea that that is going to happen?" the king asked.

With frustration in her voice, she replied, "I've already told you, Father. He is never home, he's so angry, and I don't even know why!"

"Okay, Princess. Settle down. Calm yourself," the king said. "There is always hope, no matter how grim the situation may seem and feel. To begin, you do not know what is going on with him, right? You said so yourself."

"Well, that's right. I have absolutely no idea."

"Good. Remember what you just said—you have no idea."

"Why is that important to remember?" the princess asked. "How can I forget? I have been puzzled for a long time."

"Princess, have you attempted to talk to the prince about this?"

"Well, of course I have, and I never get anywhere with him. That's when he gets angry and leaves. I try to talk to him about his behavior."

"And just what is the behavior that you are trying to talk to him about?" the king probed.

"Well, you know, his anger and … Dad, are you even listening to me? Because I do believe I have gone through all this at least twice with you and a million times in my own mind. Nobody ever listens to me anymore. Does anybody really care?"

"Princess, where did that come from?"

"From inside—where else? Dad, I am so frustrated, I don't know what to do."

"Calm down, sweetie. I have every bit of confidence we will come to a great understanding about all this."

"Good, because I sure don't understand him."

"I did not say *him*," the king clarified. "I said *this*."

"Dad, what is the difference? *Him*, *this*—it is all the same problem."

"No, my sweet. It is not all the same problem."

"Oh, Dad, don't make this hard for me. Just cut to the core. What are you talking about? I just want help."

"Do you really?"

"Yes, that is why I am here. Now I'm getting frustrated with you!"

"You are? Good. Now we are making progress."

"Oh, I get it. You are on his side. He has been here to talk to you behind my back. My own father turned traitor! Father, how could you? When did he come? How many times has he been here? Oh, man, I just don't believe this! I come for help, and instead I lose any hope I have in saving my marriage!"

"Princess!"

"Forget it, Dad. I can do this on my own. I'll figure this all out, and if he leaves me, so what! It won't be the first time something like this has happened to someone. It will be my first, but I guess no one really cares anyway. I'll talk to you later, Dad. Thanks."

The princess started to leave the room, but the king stepped in front of her to block her exit. "Hold on, Prissy. You are not going anywhere!"

"Now, Dad, don't you try to use force. I'm all grown up now, remember?"

"Princess, please sit down and listen to me for a while. I have listened to you and asked questions to help you, and look at the state you are in. Do you really think I'm not on your side? I love you with all my heart. And I know you know that. Please sit down and listen. Not just with your head but with your heart."

The princess sat down, buried her face in her hands, and began to sob. "Oh, Father, forgive me. I know I have not been myself for such a long time."

"Hmm, that's interesting. That is exactly what the prince said about you."

"He has? What else has he said?"

"Do you really want to know?" he asked.

281

"Why, of course I do. That's why I've come."

"No, Princess, you came to get help, not to find out what the prince said."

"Well, actually, Father, I did come to find out what he said. You see, he left one day in a huff. I knew he was going to be gone for some time, and so I followed him here. I was glad to find him here. It did give me hope. So, in truth, I did come to find out what he had to say to you."

"Things are starting to clear up quite nicely," the king said. "Princess, are you now ready to listen?"

The princess bowed her head and said, "Go ahead, Father. I'm ready."

"Okay, let's begin. The problem as you see it is one of anger and the prince's being gone all the time. Is that correct?"

"Well, basically. There is more, but that is the big one."

"Sweetie, do you really know that I am on your side, that I really love you, and that I want with all my heart to help?"

"Yes, Father, I do. I love you too, and I am sorry for the way I have been acting. I have just been so frustrated."

"Now, do you trust my love enough to know that what I am going to say is for your good and will be truly the best advice I can give?"

"Yes, Father. It scares me a little to hear this preface to your words, but I do know you love me. I'm ready to listen. I don't want to go back to the way it has been; I am really ready for help."

"Good. Change is often hard. It is harder on some than others. I am glad you are truly ready for change; it is time. The way you know it is time for a change is when you feel that staying the same is just not an option and you are really ready to look at the problem. You are ready now.

"When life gets uncomfortable," he continued, "and we are ready for change, often by this time our vision is so clouded by our despair that we truly don't know the direction to take. Even if help is staring us in the face, we do not see it because of our despair. We only see the darkness. This is the time we call out for help. But often, like a child in a bad dream crying out for help, when help arrives, the child is so involved in the fight that he even begins to fight the help, as you did today. The battle is over, Princess. Choose to stop fighting the battle you see. The prince is not the enemy. The prince loves you and has been trying to help you for a long time, but you've been fighting him and yourself. The true enemy is the anger you hold inside."

"Oh, Father, no. It was the prince who had the anger. He started it all."

"No, Princess. You cannot see in someone else something that is not inside of you. In fact, the only way to recognize a character trait in others is to have it within yourself. This principle works for both the positive and the negative. You see, Princess, your life is a mirror, and it reflects back to you all that you have inside. When you let go of your anger and your absence from the Prince, the problem will disappear."

"But Father, I have never left him!"

"Oh, really? Think about it. How might there be a way that you have left the prince?"

"I never have, Father—really!"

"Look at it differently, Princess. How did you leave him?"

"Hmm ...," pondered the princess. "Oh my goodness, I think I get it! I did not leave him physically, as I saw him leave me. But I left him in other ways. Oh no, Dad!"

She began to cry.

"I left him! I left him emotionally! When we began to have the children, I got so busy with them. I mean, they depended on me for their every need, and the prince—I figured he was a big boy so he could fend for himself. Dad, I was not there for him. He needed me just as I need him now."

"Yes, Princess, yes. I am so proud that you could see this so quickly."

"But what about the anger? I still don't understand that."

"Well, think of the times you were angry."

"Oh, man, there have been a lot of those times."

"Well, now, that was easy," the king replied.

"It may be easy, but it is still not clear. I had anger, but I don't get the connection."

"Often, we hold feelings deep within us—feelings that reside at our core and that were registered early in our life's experience. When you have a life experience that resonates at the same frequency as a core feeling, these feelings grow in intensity and frequency; thus, we become angrier. Anger becomes easier and easier to bring to the surface, and it is magnified upon use. Anything in our life is magnified upon use. It doesn't matter what it is."

"Well, how do you know that this anger is a core problem?" the princess asked.

"Core problems become easy to recognize in life because they become our patterns. For as long as I have known you, and that is from the beginning, you have had this pattern going. You have managed it throughout the years—until recently. It has begun to scream for you to pay attention to the problem and make a change. That is how they work. When our problems become very magnified, we then choose to look at them. Having the problem in front of you, you looked at it. Even though you were unable to recognize the source of the problem, you saw the problem. That is always so—we always see the problem. We do not always know its source. So you came to me for help, and now the problem is identified, as well as the source."

"Well, you sound as if we are done, but I do not feel done! What am I to do about this?"

"Once the problem is identified, which is usually the hardest part for most people—seeing things within themselves—the rest is a bit easier. The second step is to let it go. I mean, why would you want to hold on to something that is causing you so much grief? Just let it go."

"You make it sound like all I have to do is open my hand and let it go."

"Good visual, honey. Go for it."

"Come on, Dad. How do you do it really?"

"Honest, honey. That is a really good start. Just keep in your mind what you *intend* to do, and in time it will happen. If you struggle with it, come back and I can help you further," the king said.

"Wow, I feel as if a weight has just been lifted off my shoulders," the princess said.

"See, honey, you have started to let go already because you are feeling light. Holding onto things that bring us pain will only keep us in pain. Let go and forgive yourself and forgive your sweet prince. He loves you so much."

The princess again began to cry. "Oh, Dad, I made such a mess of things, and I hurt him so badly."

"Honey, this is where the forgiveness comes in," the king said. "If you had known all of this from the beginning, you would not have done it. It's okay; we all have wonderful life experiences from which to learn. Remember, life is a lesson in choice, a time to learn. Did you learn anything?"

"Oh, yes, and I am sure I am not finished."

"I am glad to hear that because when we do finish, Father calls us home, and I am not quite ready to let you go. You still have my grandchildren to raise."

The princess rushed over and gave her father a big hug. They heard a knock at the door.

The king answered the door and said, "Princess, there is someone who loves you very much waiting to see you."

She gasped, "Really?"

She turned and in walked the prince. She looked at him, and he smiled. She ran to him and they embraced.

"Oh, honey, will you forgive me?" she cried.

"Yes, if you will forgive me and all my learning mishaps," he answered.

And thus we have an end and a great new beginning.

32

Castle in the Clouds

The objective of this story is to help you discover and understand that connecting to your divine nature and to God is the source of true joy.

Once upon a time, not long ago, a beautiful princess lived with her handsome prince. They lived happily in their castle in the sky. They took daily walks through their garden of clouds. While they walked, they would form the clouds into unique shapes for the children who lived below to see and enjoy. The royal couple took great pleasure in this service, for they could see the children watching each day, waiting for the new shapes to appear. The children were so captivated by the clouds. It was such a simple thing, but it brought them much delight.

The prince and princess would observe the children spending hours looking at their creations. But sometimes the children would fall asleep and slumber the entire afternoon away. This concerned the royal couple. They wondered what they could do to help the children stay awake.

"They are missing so many of our beautiful creations as they dream away the afternoon," the princess sighed.

"Well, we could water the garden, and that would awaken them," replied the prince.

"Yes," she agreed, "I suppose we could, but then they would run away. What if we just clapped our hands loudly like thunder and withheld the rain?"

"Okay," agreed the prince. "Let's try it."

So they clapped loudly, waking up the sleeping children. They looked up at the sky and hurried home even though there was no rain.

"Well, that didn't work. Now what?" inquired the princess.

"Maybe it is time to move the castle again. There are so many other children in the world we could visit and serve," the prince proposed.

"No," said the princess. "I have grown so fond of these."

"You know that children do grow up and change," said the prince.

"I know, but then they have children and there are more. There are always more children to look at the clouds."

287

"I know!" said the prince, as his mind caught hold of a great idea. "Why don't we change our shapes and develop new ones? Shapes that look like the things they love. The children are growing and changing; some don't even come out to play anymore. Most of them just stay in their houses all day."

"They do?" asked the princess. "How could they when we have such a great garden of clouds for them to view?"

"Well, it is true. I've watched them very carefully," said the prince.

"What are they doing inside?" the princess asked. "How could whatever they are doing even compare to what is in the world of nature? I mean, it is not just our garden of clouds; it's everything our good king has provided for their joy and pleasure—like the bugs, the plants, all the great trees to climb, and the rocks. I have always felt that, had I not chosen to be a Cloud Princess, I would choose rocks. Rocks are so great. What remarkable colors and shapes they have. There is such diversity in rocks. I just don't understand. What could be better than the world of nature? What could be better than our world?"

"The children are missing more than the clouds, bugs, and the trees in their life," the prince said thoughtfully. "They are missing love."

"They are? And how do you know this?" the princess inquired skeptically.

"Haven't your heard the old saying? It goes like this:

'A child who grows up in love,

Has eyes cast to the clouds above,

But a child who grows up in sorrow and pain,

Has eyes cast down and they are filled with rain.'

"So that's why the children don't see our beautiful creations?" asked the princess.

"Yes," answered the prince sorrowfully. "The children's eyes are down; they are unable to see beauty because they feel so sad and alone."

"Oh, no! What can we do?"

After a brief pause, the princess cried, "I know! Let's spell words with our clouds. Let's spell 'I love you'!"

The prince chuckled. "Well, that would certainly get some attention, but you know we can't. We have laws we follow, and I think sending written messages is prohibited in one of them."

"Hmm ... yes, I guess you're right," agreed the princess. "So what can we do?"

"I think we should report this to the king and trust in his wisdom."

So the young couple hastily prepared for their journey to report their problem to the king. They arrived at the grand castle and arranged a meeting with him. He was so pleased to see them, yet he grew disheartened listening to their report.

"Yes," said the king. "I have had many such reports from my heirs in other kingdoms. The children are simply not responding to the pleasures of nature. They have forgotten the joy that it can bring."

"Do you have a solution, then?" they asked.

"Certainly," said the king. "Let's bring the children home to us."

"Oh, my," said the princess. "How could that solve the problem? That would make the parents so sad."

"Yes," said the wise king, "but sadness is not always a bad thing. Sadness comes; sadness goes. When the sadness lifts, so do their eyes, and then they could see and enjoy your garden again."

"This will not work!" protested the princess.

"Oh, I see," mused the king. "You want me to leave the children sad in their homes?"

"Well, no, but I don't want them called home early because I'm complaining," she replied. "I just want them to feel joy."

"Oh, so you thought it was your clouds that gave them joy? Because you saw them take delight in your clouds, you thought they were the source of their joy."

"Well, yes," said the princess. "I saw them become very happy when they observed our clouds."

"Princess, please sit down for a moment," said the king. "Allow me teach you a very important lesson. You're right in one sense: your clouds add to the joy of the children, just as the rocks, the bugs, and all of nature. But nothing in nature is the source of their joy."

"It is not?" the princess asked.

"No, my child. It is not," said the king. "The source of the children's joy is just that."

"Just what?"

"Just that—the Source."

"Huh?"

"Joy comes from God—the Source. As the children, as well as all of mankind, are connected to the Source or to God, they feel joy. It has nothing to do with what is on the outside, what is around them, or what is keeping them from your clouds. It is an internal spiritual crisis that they are experiencing."

"Then …," said the princess sadly, "what can I do to help them?"

"You can do as God's angels do and pray for them. But their connection to God is their choice."

"But they don't even know it!" cried the princess. "They don't even know the problem! Please, your highness, let me write a message in the clouds."

The wise king smiled. "Princess, you *do* write messages in the clouds—every day, every morning, every noon, and every sunset."

"I do? How?"

"Your beautiful clouds, as with everything in nature, are a message in and of themselves. It is a message of God's love for all mankind. Throughout the history of the earth, it has been so and will continue to be so until the end.

"My sweet princess and my goodly prince," the king continued, "how I love you both for the service you render.

Do not be dismayed. There are those who still look up and feel joy in your gift. As these children and all of humanity are awakened to their true nature and to the source of their joy, they too will look up at your garden of clouds and feel joy because your gift will remind them of God's love."

"I love you two. Now go and continue your glorious work."

The royal couple left the presence of the wise old king and returned to their garden in the sky, content. They continued to paint and create emblems of God's love for the children of men and to pray for them as the angels, and they did so happily ever after.

33

The Whispering of the Wind

The objective of this story is to teach us that our greatest moment of choice is when we are in the heat of the moment; we can choose to see the good or the bad. Our feelings do not determine our choices, but our choices will determine how we feel.

Once upon a time, a long time ago, there lived an elderly gentleman named Tabius. Tabius was old at the time this story took place. He lived in an ancient castle way up north, where the wind constantly blew.

Tabius was a kindly gentleman, and everyone who knew him loved him. People from all around would travel far to be in his presence. His wisdom was that of a sage. Tabius knew many of life's secrets. He knew how to be happy, and he also knew the secret of making those around him happy. He would sit patiently with his visitors, listening to their ways, their tales, and their questions.

The people loved him, and Tabius loved the people. Tabius was elderly, his family all grown up and departed. But he was never lonely, for his home was always full of his traveling guests. He would sit by the hour near his grand old stone fireplace, listening to the wind howl outside and making up stories about the old wind.

The wind was his friend. It had served him much during his lifetime. Generally, people don't like the wind, but Tabius had grown to value it, for he knew of its great service to mankind. He would tell his guests how wonderful the wind was, rehearsing stories of the wind in far distant lands. He would tell of the wind's gifts to man, such as the beautiful carvings the wind made with stone. He spoke of how in times of war the winds would whip the sand to protect God's warriors, acting as a cover and a shield to hide them from their enemies. He told stories of how the wind helped sailors move quickly across the vast waters and saved many sailors from an untimely death. He spoke of the wind moving great mounds of earth. The wind would sweep down and pick up the topsoil from one place and move it to other places in need of it. He told stories of how the wind would carry messages for the ancient warriors to protect them from their enemies. Yes, Tabius had many stories about the wind. His visitors loved to hear them all, over and over again.

One particular story was about the time that Tabius himself was caught in a windstorm. He was out gathering his goats and sheep from high off the mountain graze, when all of a sudden a vast wind blew in. The wind knew Tabius was his friend, yet he decided to test his strength and loyalty to see if he truly meant all the kind things he told the people.

The wind whipped furiously, scaring his goats and sheep. Tabius knew his mountain well and took his herd into a cove of rocks for protection. His faithful dog gathered quickly, under Tabius's order, his entire herd. They gathered all but one, an old favorite of Tabius. It was Toona, his she-goat.

Tabius knew of Toona's affinity for the taller grass high up by the cliffs, so he ventured out to find her. The wind was fierce. Rain had begun to fall and, with the combination of the two, felt like bullets against his face. He walked into the wind, up the mountain to find his Toona.

He knew that she would be frightened, and he feared that the strength of the wind would blow her right off the cliffs.

He talked to the wind kindly as he forged his way up the mountain, for Tabius, in his wisdom, knew the wind was just playing a trick on him to test his loyalty. Tabius asked the wind to please allow Toona to keep her life, yet if this was not to be, he would accept with sorrow her fate.

Tabius rounded the rocks where he felt Toona would be. Sure enough, she was there, pushing herself with all her might against the rocks for safety.

Tabius called to her, and in great relief Toona turned to him. Just as she did so, the wind whipped more furiously, caught her off guard, and blew her off the edge.

Tabius screamed in anguish, "No!" He fell to the ground and wept bitterly. "Why? Why would you do this to me? I was so close. She felt she was safe, and this security brought her death."

He cried, the wind still beating furiously against him, "I have been your friend all these years, telling people of your gifts to them, and this is how you repay me. I don't understand. Please teach me, for truly I do not understand!"

Tabius in his anguish was still teachable. He sought for understanding of that which had brought his Toona to her death. The master of the wind was amazed at the greatness of Tabius's character, for in his hour of trial, he still wanted to learn.

"Tabius," a voice called to him. "Tabius."

Tabius listened. Was it the wind, or was the voice in his head?

"Tabius," the voice called again.

Puzzled, Tabius answered, "Yes?"

"Tabius, you have just learned a great lesson," the voice said.

"What lesson is that? All I feel is sorrow at the fate of my poor little Toona. She trusted me, and then in that moment when she felt she was safe, she was swept to her death."

"Tabius, remember all the stories you told people about the gifts of the wind?"

"Yes, I delight in helping people find the good in the very thing that tries them the most, and up here the wind is truly a great trial for the people. Hearing about good things the wind does helps them to handle the burden of living here. This is a very difficult place to live because of the fierce winds. The wind here has caused death and sorrow to the people and their loved ones. So I try to help ease their burdens by having them focus on the good, not the bad."

"That is the very reason the people love you so, Tabius. It is because you help them feel better about their trials and their lives. What now would you tell someone if they had come to you with this sad tale?"

"I do not know, for I am now in the heat of my anguish and I can't think clearly. You tell me."

"No, Tabius. I cannot do that. You would miss the very point of the lesson I am trying to teach you."

"Oh, let me be. Let me be in my anguish for a time. I truly cannot think, and I have not the strength to be wise and patient. I need to get back to my herd. If you want to help me, turn down the wind so I can get back safely."

"No, Tabius. That is not the way. That is not the help you need."

"It feels like the help I need. Do you know how long I have had Toona? She was my first she-goat. She was the beginning of my herd. I can't tell you how many goats in my herd came from her. She was so gentle and good. Yes, she had a wandering streak, but going for the best grass gave her incredible strength. Why did Toona have to die?" Tabius turned his head toward the rocks and wept.

"Tabius, listen to the wind. It is calling to you."

Tabius turned slightly, lifting his head to hear the message of the wind.

"Tabius, I love you, and I love all that you have done for me. I love all the stories you tell about me and all the good that you do in my behalf. But Tabius, the wind, like all of life, has its opposite. It has good and bad. The wind can serve and destroy, as you well know from the stories you tell. But the wind's purpose is not to bring good or bad into the lives of the people. The purpose of the wind is to provide man another element of choice. It is here, in this moment, that you will decide Toona's fate."

"What?" Tabius asked. "Toona is already dead, swept off. There is no way she could survive that great fall."

"I am not talking about her death. I am talking about her gift to your life."

"You said *fate*. I understand that to be her outcome. She is already dead. What's the point?"

"You are angry with me."

"No … I mean, *yes*! Yes, I am angry with you. I was so close—so close—and you took her!"

"Tabius, what is it you want of me?" the wind whispered.

"I want to know why you took Toona. Why would you do that to me? I am your greatest friend. I help people see the good in all you do, and they love it. They love how it makes them feel. It gives them strength to go another day."

"Then why would you not give this gift, this very service, to yourself? Why can't you look to the good in this experience?"

"I cannot see it because of my sorrow," Tabius answered. "I can only feel now."

"Tabius, here is your moment, your greatest moment of choice. Yes, you are feeling great sorrow, but you can also in this moment choose to look at the good or the bad. Your feelings do not determine your choice; your choice will determine your feelings."

Tabius heard that. He also felt the truth of it in his heart. *Yes*, he thought, *this is my moment to choose.*

"I will choose to honor Toona and all the gifts she has given me. She has given me my herd, or at least a great portion of it. I will name my greatest goat in the herd for her. Whether it is a he- or a she-goat, the name will be Toona in honor of her. And as long as I live, there will always be a Toona in the herd."

"Yes! Now how do you feel?"

"I feel so much better. I am going to miss her, but she lived a good long while. She was very old, and I am grateful for our times together."

"Yes, Tabius, that is good. Toona's life now will be looked upon as a life of giving, not a death of tragedy."

Tabius, strengthened and feeling lighter, returned to his herd. He was wrapped up in his thoughts of Toona's life, not the tragedy of her death. And in this very critical time, he felt at peace.

Yes, this story of the wind he would always remember. It would be a time on which he would reflect again and again as he told others the story of his beloved Toona.

Tabius truly became an example to the people when they all heard his tragedy and witnessed his strength. Tabius on that day was given his greatest gift from the wind. He was given the opportunity to choose peace instead of sorrow and to live the life he taught.

34
Leah's Lesson

The objective of this story is to illustrate that we are all children of royal birth, our Father is king over heaven and earth. The path to becoming all we were meant to be, is paved with gratitude for our life's most difficult trials.

Once upon a time, not long ago, there lived a beautiful fairy princess. She lived in a beautiful fairy kingdom in the woods. She was a kind and loving princess, as all fairy princesses are. Her name was Leah.

Leah loved to dance. She especially loved to dance in the light of the early morning dawn and by the light of the moon. She danced the moment spring dropped her first kiss upon the earth and in autumn's first frost. This fairy princess just loved to dance.

Each morning, no matter the time or season of the year, she could be found dancing through the forest glades. Such joy she felt as her wings took flight! Her arms and legs moved like crystal snowflakes floating magically through the air.

Leah loved life. She loved waking up to each new day and doing the work her father assigned her to do. But most of all she loved being herself. She knew things about herself that few fairies realized. She knew that she indeed was a princess, and she knew her father was the king. Now this may sound a little strange to say about a fairy princess, so allow me to explain.

Every fairy born is a princess or a prince, yet not all know this. The title of princess or prince is magically bestowed when the fairies themselves perceive the wonder. This magic happens the moment they realize this. Becoming a prince or princess is a process of growth; it doesn't happen all at once.

Fairies are born into families, just as you and I. Their families are similar to ours in that they learn, grow, and experience life. They have adventures and trials just as we do. They have many experiences in the fairy realm, doing the things fairies do. They are subject to laws and have responsibilities as we do. Yet one of the most significant similarities is that they too have royal parentage. The biggest differences between the human family and the fairy family are their size and of course their ability to fly.

The fairies are very close to nature. Mankind at one time was as close to nature as the fairies, but time and circumstances have changed all that. But this is not what my story is about; it is about a princess who knew she was a princess.

My intention in telling you Leah's story is to help you learn the true nature of your being and to help you discover, as she did, just who you are.

Leah grew up in a beautiful home located at the edge of the glade. She had brothers, sisters, and extended family who lived nearby. She went to school with all the young fairies, but there was something very different about her from the beginning.

When Leah was very young, her mother spent a great deal of time with her talking to her and playing with her, as she did with all of her brothers and sisters. Her mother would often read to her from the best books. The family spent a great deal of time working and playing together.

Leah had a great, curious mind and asked a thousand and one questions a day. Her mother was grateful she was not an only child and that her brothers and sisters could often spend time with her to help satisfy her thirsting curiosity. This gave her mother a chance to get other things done.

One particular day as Leah danced in the glade, she caught a glimpse of someone whisking by. She thought perhaps it was a young prince. She was very surprised at this for she believed she was alone. She saw him whip to another hiding place as she swirled and danced. Seeing this, she immediately stopped and called out, "Who's there? I saw you, so you might as well come out. I know you are there."

Soon she saw a red-faced young man come out from behind a large boulder.

"Hello," he said shyly. "My name is Tuck."

"Well, I can see why your parents might have named you such, tucking behind the rocks like that. My name is Leah. Why were you hiding?"

Tuck bowed his head, embarrassed. "I was watching you dance, and I felt that if you saw me, you would stop and I did not want you to stop. I love watching you dance. Never before have I witnessed such beauty and grace. I am sorry."

"Sorry for what?" Leah asked.

"Sorry I got caught, for indeed you stopped dancing."

Leah smiled. Tuck smiled back.

"Well, Tuck, it is not polite to spy. You know that, don't you?"

"Why, certainly. That is why I was trying so hard not to get caught. But as you danced you were moving farther and farther away, and I had to keep you in sight."

"You had to?"

"Yes, I come here often to watch you dance. Your movement inspires me. For you see, I love to dance as well."

Leah smiled. "Oh, you do?"

"Yes, I have been dancing for years. I found this place quite by accident and decided that when I had a spare moment I would return here to dance. Well, the day I returned, I found you here dancing. Your dancing inspired me so I could not interrupt. I could only watch in awe."

Leah blushed. "Well, the glade is open to everyone. we could have shared."

"No, that is quite all right. I enjoyed every bit of it, except getting caught. Now I believe that part wasn't so bad either. I'm finally getting to meet you."

"Finally?" Leah asked. "How long have you been watching me dance?"

"Oh, about a month," Tuck admitted.

"Now I'm the one who is embarrassed. Who knows what I could have done in that time! Tuck, that was mean of you to not let me know you were there."

"I'm sorry, Leah. I know it was unkind, but I did not want it to end and I did not want you to stop."

Leah did not know what to say. She was mad and flattered all at the same time. "I will forgive you if you promise never to hide again. And I feel it only fair now for me to get to see you dance."

Leah placed herself squarely on top of the boulder and folded her arms in preparation for her private show. Tuck was surprised at her boldness, yet he did feel he owed it to her, so off he flew.

Leah was immediately taken by his strength and skill. She was stunned! She watched him dance for an hour, yet it seemed like only a minute. He returned to her.

"There. Are we even?"

"Aaaa ... no," Leah said. "I think I have twenty-nine days left." They both laughed. "Yes, I'll let you off the hook with that. You are brilliant!"

"And so are you."

Leah smiled. "Tuck, it's getting late. I'd better get back."

"May I meet you here again sometime?" Tuck asked.

She smiled. "Tuck, I hardly know you. Maybe we will get to meet again sometime. Thank you." Leah nodded her head and off she flew. *Wow*, she thought. *Boy, would I like to meet you again. But first I have to get over this mad and embarrassed feeling.*

Tuck was surprised. Surely he had made a better impression on her than that. Puzzled but hopeful, he left for home.

Leah returned home and quickly flew to her mother to tell her of the events. "Mom, I'm so embarrassed and so mad! What shall I do?"

"Leah, you know the right thing to do. Look for the good in this situation. Yes, it was hard, and yes, you were embarrassed to find that someone had been watching you for so long. It was not proper on Tuck's part to hide like that. I can understand your feelings. But answer me this: do you like the way you feel now, mad and embarrassed?"

"No, not at all."

"Then choose to feel differently. Leah, you are in charge of your feelings, and you are in charge of how quickly you learn your lessons. What have you learned from this experience?"

"Hmm," she pondered. "Well, I guess that being sneaky does not feel good to the person you are sneaking on."

"And?"

"Forgiveness feels better than anger and embarrassment."

"And?"

"I may have found a wonderful dancing partner."

"Good for you, Leah. Can you think of anything else?"

"No. Help me, Mom. Is there anything else?"

"Yes. Leah, there is a lot more to see in this lesson, but I do not want to keep you from the experience of learning and discovering it. You chew on it a bit and try to come up with more. Then tonight after dinner we will go outside and visit again."

"Ah, thanks, Mom! You are so great. I love you so much."

"Leah, it is easy to be a great mom when you have great kids."

"Leah pondered the situation for several more hours. She had quite a great list to report to her mother that evening when they sat together.

She had gained a great deal of growth from this lesson. And in the end, Tuck indeed became her forever dancing partner.

Leah's journey to become a princess continued on with each daily step of learning from her every life experience and making good thought choices. This experience accelerated her growth in such a way that it all became very clear.

When your thoughts are in line with truth, it is only natural to see who you truly are. You are a child of royal birth. You are a child of God.

I prayed,

"Heavenly Father, I don't know how to make the changes I desire."

He answered,

"Think only upon that which you want."